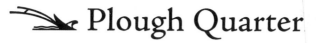 # Plough Quarter

BREAKING GROUND FOR A RENEWED

Autumn 2019, Number 22

Artists: Dean Mitchell, Mark Freear, Timothy Jones, Paweł Filipczak, Mary Pal, Harley Manifold, Sami Lalu Jahola, Marc Chagall, Russell Bain

Plough Quarterly

WWW.PLOUGH.COM

Meet the community behind *Plough*

Plough Quarterly is published by the Bruderhof, an international community of families and singles seeking to follow Jesus together. Members of the Bruderhof are committed to a way of radical discipleship in the spirit of the Sermon on the Mount. Inspired by the first church in Jerusalem (Acts 2 and 4), they renounce private property and share everything in common in a life of nonviolence, justice, and service to neighbors near and far. The community includes people from a wide range of backgrounds. There are twenty-three Bruderhof settlements in both rural and urban locations in the United States, England, Germany, Australia, and Paraguay, with around 3,000 people in all.

To learn more or arrange a visit, see the community's website at *bruderhof.com.*

Plough Quarterly features original stories, ideas, and culture to inspire everyday faith and action. Starting from the conviction that the teachings and example of Jesus can transform and renew our world, we aim to apply them to all aspects of life, seeking common ground with all people of goodwill regardless of creed. The goal of *Plough Quarterly* is to build a living network of readers, contributors, and practitioners so that, in the words of Hebrews, we may "spur one another on toward love and good deeds."

Plough Quarterly includes contributions that we believe are worthy of our readers' consideration, whether or not we fully agree with them. Views expressed by contributors are their own and do not necessarily reflect the editorial position of *Plough* or of the Bruderhof communities.

Editor: Peter Mommsen. Senior Editors: Veery Huleatt, Sam Hine. Editor-at-Large: Caitrin Keiper. Managing Editor: Shana Goodwin. Associate Editors: Susannah Black, Maureen Swinger, Ian Barth. International Editions: Daniel Hug (German), Chungyon Won (Korean), Allen Page (French).
Designers: Rosalind Stevenson, Miriam Burleson. Creative Director: Clare Stober. Copy Editors: Wilma Mommsen, Mary Catherine Ausman. Fact Checker: Emmy Barth Maendel. Marketing Director: Trevor Wiser.
Founding Editor: Eberhard Arnold (1883–1935)

Plough Quarterly No. 22: Vocation
Published by Plough Publishing House, ISBN 978-0-87486-322-2
Copyright © 2019 by Plough Publishing House. All rights reserved.

Scripture quotations (unless otherwise noted) are from the New Revised Standard Version Bible, copyright © 1989 the Division of Christian Education of the National Council of the Churches of Christ in the United States of America. Used by permission. All rights reserved.

Front cover: *Sanitation Worker* by Dean Mitchell; image used with permission. Back cover: *Autumn on the Loch,* photograph by Russell Bain; image used with permission. Inside front cover: *Campfire* by Mark Freear; image used with permission.

Editorial Office	*Subscriber Services*	*United Kingdom*	*Australia*
151 Bowne Drive	PO Box 345	Brightling Road	4188 Gwydir Highway
Walden, NY 12586	Congers, NY 10920-0345	Robertsbridge	Elsmore, NSW
T: 845.572.3455	T: 800.521.8011	TN32 5DR	2360 Australia
info@plough.com	*subscriptions@plough.com*	T: +44(0)1580.883.344	T: +61(0)2.6723.2213

Plough Quarterly (ISSN 2372-2584) is published quarterly by Plough Publishing House, PO Box 398, Walden, NY 12586.
Individual subscription $32 / £24 / €28 per year. Subscribers outside the United Kingdom and European Union pay in US dollars.
Periodicals postage paid at Walden, NY 12586 and at additional mailing offices.
POSTMASTER: Send address changes to *Plough Quarterly,* PO Box 345, Congers, NY 10920-0345.

Photo by Krzysztof Kowalik / Unsplash

Why We Work

PETER MOMMSEN

Dear Reader,

AS A NEWCOMER to Germany, I wasn't prepared for the roofers' guild uniform. Several of the men in my work crew were wearing it despite the scorching August sun: white shirt, eight-button vest, black corduroy bell-bottoms with carpenter's-rule pockets and conspicuous double zippers. "Normal guys wear this?" I asked myself as I carried stacks of ceramic tiles up to where a gable was being restored. Even in my T-shirt and jeans, it was hot work, done at a brisk pace, without much banter.

It was 2004, and my wife and I, newly married, had arrived in Dresden from New York a few days before. We were living with a friend who was renovating his century-old villa, and I offered to help the roofing contractors over the summer. From what I'd seen of roofing firms at home, I expected a corner-cutting outfit staffed with poorly trained employees laboring for low pay. Instead, I found myself working with a family firm – masters, journeymen, and apprentices – who clearly pitied anyone who wasn't a roofer. Even for a non-roofer, it was convincing.

It's not that the crew's working relationships were all cheerful camaraderie, or that the pay was particularly good. Journeymen in the area, I'd learn, typically earned only seven to eight euros an hour (nine to ten US dollars), even before taxes. But the roofers had pride: in hard work, in a job done to demanding standards, in a trade with its own dignity and traditions. To these men, honor belonged to those sweating up on the scaffolding, not to the white-collar professionals whose homes they built or repaired. On the construction site, the hierarchy of capitalism temporarily flipped: the craftsman, not the customer, was king. It takes a VIP, after all, to have the nerve to wear double-zipper bell-bottoms.

These roofers came to mind as I was reading *Bullshit Jobs*, a recent book by David Graeber, professor of anthropology at the London School of Economics. According to Graeber, a large portion of today's jobs involve tasks that the employees themselves consider pointless. He reports that in a 2015 YouGov poll, 37 percent of Britons said that their job does not make a meaningful contribution to the world; in another survey, 40 percent of Dutch workers similarly believed that their jobs had no good reason to exist. What are these socially useless jobs? Most of them, Graeber says, involve administrative, managerial, clerical, service, and sales functions such as telemarketing: sectors of the job market that, combined, ballooned from a quarter of total employment in 1910 to three-quarters in 2000. Using dozens of in-depth interviews, Graeber argues that workers who believe their jobs are worthless are probably correct.

Whether or not Graeber's overall thesis holds up, his interviewees give powerful expression to a hunger that seems to be growing around the developed world: a desire for work that has meaning and purpose. According to a 2018 study of US workers by the Harvard Business Review, nine out of ten respondents said they would be willing to sacrifice income in order for their work to be more meaningful; just

The black guild uniform for German woodworkers, including roofers, goes back to the nineteenth century.

one out of twenty considered their jobs to be as meaningful as they could be. The study's authors cast this finding as a management opportunity: if you can make employees feel as if their work has meaning – bring on those socially conscious projects and sustainability competitions! – they'll be willing to work more for less.

Marx described the alienation of the industrial proletariat from their work; this new alienation afflicts white-collar workers as well. Claudio Oliver, a farmer in Curitiba, Brazil, told me how dozens of professionals, most in their twenties, come each month to visit the urban garden and bakery he helped start. What is the profile of the people who come to him? "It's typically a young man or woman who goes to that office-cubicle job one day and looks out the window to where the landscaping crew is working and realizes, 'Wow, I wish I were the guy down there driving the lawnmower instead of doing this.'" Many of the visitors end up taking a sabbatical of a few weeks or months to learn to grow vegetables, raise goats, and bake sourdough; several have become permanent members of the community that runs the farm.

VOCATION, "CALLING," is the answer that Protestant Christianity gives when asked what gives our work meaning. Vocation sums up one of the Reformation's signature ideas: that each person is called by God to serve the common good in a particular line of work. Today it's a staple theme of Christian authors, youth pastors, life coaches, and conferences: "Everyone has a God-given calling. What's yours?" Your vocation, evidently, might be almost anything: as a nurse, a wilderness guide, a calligrapher, a missionary, an activist, a venture capitalist, a politician . . .

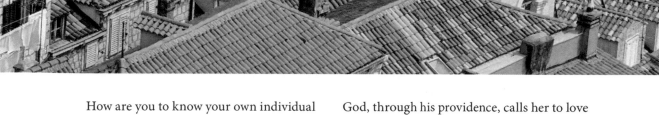

How are you to know your own individual vocation? "A calling is simply a tug on our hearts by God toward a particular thing," advises *Relevant* magazine. "Follow your passion," recommends the online publication *Theology of Work*, adopting a secular motto. A more poetic way of saying the same thing comes from the Presbyterian theologian Frederick Buechner: vocation, he writes in his 1973 book *Wishful Thinking: A Theological ABC*, is "the place where your deep gladness and the world's deep hunger meet."

It sounds as good as falling in love. Vocation: the jolt you feel as you walk past that special stand at the college career fair – all to the greater glory of God!

But such high-flown notions leave out the bulk of humanity. Deep gladness isn't what leads people to work as motel maids, supermarket cashiers, or call-center employees, much less sweatshop workers or migrant farm laborers. Yet each day, millions go to jobs like these. Nor is following one's passion an option for those hindered from working by disability, mental illness, or trauma. Is vocation, then, just for the able, well-educated, and well-heeled?

Not according to the Reformation's original understanding, which was both deeper and more realistic than much contemporary vocation talk. In the sixteenth century, Martin Luther began to interpret a line by the apostle Paul in a novel way: "Let every man abide in the calling wherein he was called" (1 Cor. 7:20). Luther seized on the word calling, and gave it a broader meaning than the medieval church, with its emphasis on the special callings of priests and monastics, had ever done. A person's calling, he argued, is simply to whatever station in life she finds herself in; it is her vocation because it is the place in which God, through his providence, calls her to love her neighbor. Tinker, tailor, soldier, sailor – all God-ordained vocations, and therefore of equal value. No matter how menial one's work may be, it is a sacred calling through which God works in the world. In Luther's words, "God milks the cows through the vocation of the milkmaids."

Luther's vision of vocation would prove a liberating power, giving new dignity to the labors of ordinary peasants and craftsmen. Refined by Calvin, it would reshape much of Europe; in fact, as Max Weber famously argued, the Protestant ideal of vocation, with its emphasis on a strong work ethic and ascetic dedication to the discipline of one's trade, can be credited for the flowering of capitalism.

Workers who believe their jobs are worthless are probably correct.

This is the background for why today, "vocational" schools exist to teach plumbing or welding, not spiritual practices. It's the reason why several nations' constitutions guarantee freedom of vocation as an essential aspect of human dignity. And it likely explains, through the windings of history, the pride of the corduroy-clad German roofers I worked with in Dresden. As Luther – who long made that region of Germany his home – might have put it, God builds roofs through the vocation of the roofers.

WHATEVER THE VIRTUES of the Protestant ideal of vocation, however, it has a serious flaw: as an account of New Testament teaching, it is wrong. Luther illustrates this defect most clearly by taking it to an extreme. For him, *all work,* not just farming or the trades, expresses God's will; there are many possible vocations. For example: "If you see there is a lack of hangmen . . . and you find that you are qualified, you should offer your services." He adds, "For the hand that wields this sword and kills with it is not man's hand, but God's; and it is not man, but God, who hangs, tortures, beheads, kills, and fights. All these are God's works and judgments."

No executioner, then, is left behind in this theology of vocation. Yet it's hard to imagine anything more contrary to the spirit of the Jesus of the four Gospels or, for that matter, the rest of the New Testament.

When the New Testament writers use the words translated in English as *vocation* or *calling,* they are never referring to work, much less to a particular trade or profession. As Will Willimon explains (page 14), the New Testament knows only one form of vocation: discipleship. And discipleship is far more likely to mean leaving father and mother, houses and land, than it is to mean embracing one's identity as a fisherman or tax collector. It demands the sacrifice of what we naturally desire. "When Christ calls a man," said Bonhoeffer, "he bids him come and die."

This is not a popular way to talk about vocation. Most of us would prefer to follow Luther in simply baptizing the status quo, despite any contradictions that might result. When others feel the ache of a real lack in their lives – when they sense the alienation that arises from working and living in an unjust social order – we'd rather apply the soothing salve of Christianity-lite, assuring them that all is as it should be.

But the status quo is what Christ came to abolish: "Behold, I make all things new"

> **Most of us would prefer to follow Luther in simply baptizing the status quo.**

(Rev. 21:5). In its place he brought the only true calling, to the renewed common life shaped wholly by love that he describes in the Sermon on the Mount. As David Bentley Hart put it in our summer 2019 issue titled *Beyond Capitalism:* "Christians are those . . . who are no longer at liberty to imagine or desire any social or political or economic order other than the *koinonia* of the early church, no other communal morality than the anarchy of Christian love."

This issue of *Plough* aims to build on our *Beyond Capitalism* issue by focusing on people who lived their lives with that sense of vocation. Such a life demands self-sacrifice and a willingness to recognize one's own supposed strengths as weaknesses, as it did for the Canadian moral philosopher Jean Vanier (page 43). It involves a lifelong commitment to a flesh-and-blood church, as Coptic Archbishop Angaelos describes (page 26). It may even require a readiness to give up one's life, as it did for Annalena Tonelli, an Italian humanitarian who pioneered the treatment of tuberculosis in the Horn of Africa (page 32).

But as these stories also testify, it's a vocation that brings a gladness deeper than any self-chosen path. The many in our society who protest that their work is useless are on to something: they, and we, are created for a higher meaning and purpose – for what T. S. Eliot memorably called "a condition of complete simplicity" that "cost[s] not less than everything." It's not too high a price to pay.

Warm greetings,

Peter

Peter Mommsen, *Editor*

C. S. LEWIS

A VOCATION IS a terrible thing. To be called out of nature into the supernatural life is at first (or perhaps not quite at first – the wrench of the parting may be felt later) a costly honour. Even to be called from one natural level to another is loss as well as gain. Man has difficulties and sorrows which the other primates escape. But to be called up higher still costs still more.

THÉRÈSE OF LISIEUX

I OPENED, one day, the Epistles of St. Paul to seek relief in my sufferings. My eyes fell on the twelfth and thirteenth chapters of the First Epistle to the Corinthians. I read that all cannot become Apostles, Prophets, and Doctors; that the Church is composed of different members; that the eye cannot also be the hand. The answer was clear, but it did not fulfill my desires, or give to me the peace I sought. "Then descending into the depths of my nothingness, I was so lifted up that I reached my aim" (Saint John of the Cross).

Without being discouraged I read on, and found comfort in this counsel: "Be zealous for the better gifts. And I show unto you a yet more excellent way" (1 Cor. 12:31). The Apostle then explains how all perfect gifts are nothing without Love. . . .

Then, beside myself with joy, I cried, 'O Jesus, my love, at last I have found my vocation. My vocation is love! . . . In the heart of the Church, my Mother, I will be LOVE! Thus shall I be all things."

MOTHER TERESA

OUR VOCATION is nothing else but to belong to Christ. The work that we do is only a means to put our love for Christ into living action.

All the religious congregations – nuns, priests, even the Holy Father – all have the same vocation: to belong to Jesus. "I have chosen you to be mine." That's our vocation. Our means, how we spend our time, may be different. Our love for Jesus in action is only the means, just like clothes. I wear this, you wear that: It's a means. But a vocation is not a means. Vocation, for a Christian, is Jesus.

We all have been called by God. As missionaries we must be carriers of God's love, ready to go in haste, like Mary, in search of souls; burning lights that give light to all men; the salt of the earth; souls consumed with one desire: Jesus. ➤

Sources: C. S. Lewis, *Reflections on the Psalms* (Geoffrey Bles, 1958), 131; Thérèse of Lisieux, *Story of a Soul*, trans. Thomas Taylor (Burns, Oates & Washbourne, 1912), chapter 11; Mother Teresa, *No Greater Love* (New World Library, 2016), 147.

Henri-Edmond Cross, *The Farm, Evening,* oil on canvas, 1893

Life beyond Capitalism

On Plough Quarterly's *Issue 21,* Beyond Capitalism, *Summer 2019:* Best. Plough. Ever. When *Plough Quarterly* is as brave as its Summer 2019 issue, it is truly one of the most fascinating and authentic Christian voices of our generation.

Ross Eiler, Bloomington Catholic Worker,
Bloomington, Indiana

On Peter Mommsen's "The Economics of Love," Summer 2019: This issue of *Plough* was nothing short of a prophetic voice, crying out against mammon in a crooked wilderness. Thank you.

We noticed an interesting tension between the introductory editorial which dismissed integralism, pointing to the "downsides inherent in any attempt to secure the common good through state coercion," and the point raised by David Bentley Hart, that "small intentional communities committed to some form of Christian collectivism are all very well . . . but they can also be a tremendous distraction, especially if their isolation from and simultaneous dependency upon the larger political order is mistaken for a sufficient realization of the ideal Christian polity."

Pater Edmund Waldstein, a monk who cited the Catholic Church's teaching on the state's role in securing the universal destination of goods, also noted the struggle of his own monastery to maintain itself as a Christian community within the larger system of capitalism: "The system has its own dynamic, which is hard to escape." The positive role of political power can also be noted in defending the gardens of "the Bronx Agrarian"; its absence, in the failure to defend the rights of Vietnamese "Working Girls."

For us as Catholic integralists and radical distributists, we are very interested in how intentional communities of Christian virtue can be constructed, as well as how they can relate to, blossom into, and sustain grassroots political movements. The Bruderhof is an inspiration for the community aspirations of many Catholics; we hope that our Magisterium's Social Teaching might serve in a similar manner to all people of good will.

In these turbulent times, it is inevitable that we will be driven to ask fundamental questions about politics, liberalism, and Christianity. We are certain that a future issue of *Plough* on these topics could provide valuable insight.

We would also be very interested in an issue on the practicalities of building intentional communities: how are the budgets balanced, the resources allocated, the work done, the problems solved, and the children raised? Most importantly, how do they begin, especially in a world of economic struggles for so many families and congregations of Christians who also pay homage to mammon, who have to be re-evangelized before such a possibility can even be imagined?

We are eager to read forthcoming issues: so much is required to imagine a Christian culture, economics, and politics beyond capitalism. Your work is a worthy addition.

Thomas Hackett, cofounder of the Tradistae
network, Lancaster, Pennsylvania

In his lead editorial, Mommsen poses a stark dichotomy: the "attempt to secure the common good through state coercion" versus the Radical Reformation model of purely voluntary "brotherly community," and he warns Christians against responding to the "public sin" of

---

We welcome letters to the editor. Letters and web comments may be edited for length and clarity, and may be published in any medium. Letters should be sent with the writer's name and address to letters@plough.com.

capitalism in a political way because he worries that socialist politics will end with coercion.

Although Mommsen's indictment of capitalism is eloquent and his evocation of Bruderhof life fascinating, his dichotomy is unsatisfying, and he seems to miss the point of convergence between Christianity and socialism. In biblical accounts from the covenant at Sinai to the early church, membership means choosing, but it also means having been already chosen. Voluntarism is only half the story: we cannot choose not to be born dependent and indebted; we cannot choose not to be shaped by and to have a share in shaping those around us.

Beyond the dichotomy between coercion and voluntarism, biblical texts and Jewish and Christian traditions reveal a range of ways to blur the lines between "what I will" and "what is willed by others" (or by an Other): acculturation into community, reinterpretation of tradition, mutual recognition by a community's members. From blurrings like these emerge the possibilities for human community that we in our era call democracy – including the hope of democratic socialism. Politics need not be a synonym for coercion. If voluntary communities of radical sharing like the Bruderhof are one kind of witness to what Mommsen calls "another life," might not the everyday agitation and organizing of democratic socialist politics witness to that same life in a different way?

Geoffrey Kurtz, Brooklyn, New York

The editors respond: We thank Geoffrey Kurtz and Thomas Hackett for their insightful questions. We plan to focus on the relation of faith to politics in *Plough*'s Spring 2020 issue.

Can Markets Be Moral?

On David Bentley Hart's "What Lies Beyond Capitalism?", Summer 2019: I am grateful for Hart's strident critique of an amoral approach to economics that respects neither the Creator, nor humans, nor the environment. But I am unsure whether Hart's analysis meaningfully describes capitalism at all, given that Adam Smith, the so-called father of capitalism, would also reject an amoral economics. Indeed, the argument of *The Wealth of Nations* depends on a concept that was once common among Christian treatments of economics: that of the just price. It's immoral, Smith holds, for capitalists to wield the power of the state to enrich themselves by constraining supply and elevating prices. On Smith's rendering, capitalism is a moral project.

Terminology aside, Hart does not make any concrete proposals for Christian politics today. In rejecting the materialism of capitalism, he loses sight of material realities altogether, and remains in the ethereal.

Hart rightly criticizes the unbridled desire ubiquitous in our economic order, and sees in it the contradiction of capitalism, namely, that infinite desire coupled with finite resources results in the consumption of all. One might hope not merely to limit, but to reorient our desires: to radically reform economic exchange from within by directing our consumption in accord with our true end. Instead, Hart treats an accidental feature of our economic order – the unquenchable thirst for material goods – as substantial, even as he pays little attention to material limits when it comes to the problem of how to allocate economic goods. Extreme generosity to the stranger while neglecting one's family or neighbors is injustice. In the same way, anarchy with respect to our obligations to others is not virtue, but vice. Rid the world of possessive individualism, and we must still grapple with finitude.

Hart is instructive in his reminder that "the full *koinonia* of the body of Christ is not an option to be set alongside other equally plausible alternatives." Christ is Lord over all. Yet, if we consider concrete human existence, we see that the social order is not uniform; rather, we exist as members of a multiplicity of societies with different ends. We need not reduce the church to the level of these other societies, and may instead recognize that the whole world is not the church, even as the whole world is not the family, except in an analogical sense. Communism suits the family well, and it may be fine for the church – but I fear that it might not fare so well outside it.

John Buchmann, Philadelphia, Pennsylvania

Not Our Own

On Edmund Waldstein's "Robin Hood Economics," Summer 2019: This illuminating essay raises vital wider questions about the nature of agency in an embodied and interconnected world. In positing the universal destination of goods, Waldstein asks us to consider what is – and is not – really *ours*, and the tension between what might be considered just ownership and its avaricious mirror image. On the one hand, we tend to take more responsibility for what we produce – as Aquinas himself pointed out. As creative beings, we have a special relationship with the fruits of our own labors. At the same time, the relationship we have with what we can *hoard* is fraught with the potential for sin: to amass more than what we need is not merely to commit an injustice against our fellow man but against a God who has ordered a world for the benefit of mankind, and who is the just and final owner of all property and goods alike.

But we can, and must, go further, asking these questions not merely of the economic sphere, but of all elements of public and private life. The Christian tradition challenges us to see not merely our property, but our bodies and souls, as not fully our own. If we justly own what we create, as Aquinas posited, it is because we exist *imago dei*: fundamentally belonging to our own Creator. "Robin Hood economics" is, at its core, an understanding not only of the universal destination of goods, but of souls as well.

Tara Isabella Burton, New York, New York

Why We Need a Labor Movement

On Maria Hengeveld's "Working Girls," Summer 2019: Although Hengeveld focuses on Nike and its employment of girls in Vietnam, her arguments would hold for most American and Western companies that intentionally find countries that yield cheap labor and nonexistent labor laws. The piece was well researched and well done, and I appreciated it. I do, however, have a few things I'd like to point out.

Hengeveld brings up the idea that "a bad job is better than no job," and rightly concludes that it is often used to justify any abuse related to "the conditions under which products and profits are made." It must not be used in that way. However, from the perspective of some workers, the statement is objectively true. I am an immigrant; I started working at age fourteen. When we first came to America, my parents took jobs that were not commensurate with their education, precisely because "a bad job is better than no job." When I worked at age fourteen, I didn't complain about the $3.35 minimum wage I was paid, for the same reason.

It's a reality that most poor people will accept less money and poor working conditions for the sake of having a job. And yes, that includes jobs that separate families. One woman I interviewed for my book on immigration told me of Western oil companies that brought in Bangladeshi workers to the oil rigs in Basra rather than employ the local Iraqis. They paid the Bangladeshis less, and (since a bad job is better than no job) these men left their families behind in order to work. She also lived in Dubai for a few years and observed the human suffering of many economic migrants there as well.

Poor people in poor places are paid less for their labor than better-off people in wealthier countries, but if their pay meets their local cost of living, this is not intrinsically wrong. We need to be careful not to map our ways onto others. That also applies to exporting our consumer culture. It is a good thing when wealth flows into these poorer places, but it shouldn't be coming only through Western companies doing business there. These countries are lifted up when we help them create their own products made within their own countries – the work of their hands, which they can export and share with the rest of the world.

It is also a valid concern that the money we pay for T-shirts and sneakers will end up primarily in other hands than those of the locals and workers; that the value of their labor will be extracted but that the reward for that labor will be whittled away by the time it reaches the worker. This is why strong but ethical labor movements are essential all over the world.

The labor movements here in America are a shell of what they used to be. I am keen to see a labor movement comeback. But only when the human person becomes more important than the stuff we buy will such a comeback be possible.

Luma Simms, Phoenix, Arizona

Rediscovering Ruskin

On Eugene McCarraher's "Comrade Ruskin," Summer 2019: Socialism is back. The rhetoric and ideas of class conflict have in recent years fueled the growth of social democratic parties – and even more radical movements – in the United States, the United Kingdom, and elsewhere, as well as bold policy proposals that, if enacted, would transform the economic structures of health care, education, and finance. I couldn't help but think about the contemporary political scene as I read, with interest, Eugene McCarraher's latest essay on the communism of the Victorian critic John Ruskin. This could be Ruskin's moment. After all, his invective against the abuses of the capitalist class and the world that economic elites created – a "confused wreck of social order and life" – rivals and often exceeds the most acute social criticism that the left has to offer. And maybe Ruskin's dismissal of those court intellectuals of the capitalist order would strike a chord with activists and fellow travelers who call bluff on the supposed constraints of the national debt or the assumptions of the so-called free market. Maybe.

There is, on the other hand, plenty in the work of Ruskin that chafes against the guiding assumptions of a world that, particularly on the political left, has become allergic to the language of religion. As McCarraher argues, Ruskin's vision of an economic and social order rests, in the end, on metaphysical convictions about the good life and on a decidedly Christian view of a world imbued with sacramental meaning and ends. Consider Ruskin's polemic against nineteenth-century economics. "The real science of political economy, which has yet to be distinguished from the bastard science, as medicine from witchcraft, and astronomy from astrology," Ruskin wrote, "is that which teaches nations to desire and labour for the things that lead to life: and which teaches them to scorn and destroy the things that lead to destruction."

(continued on page 102)

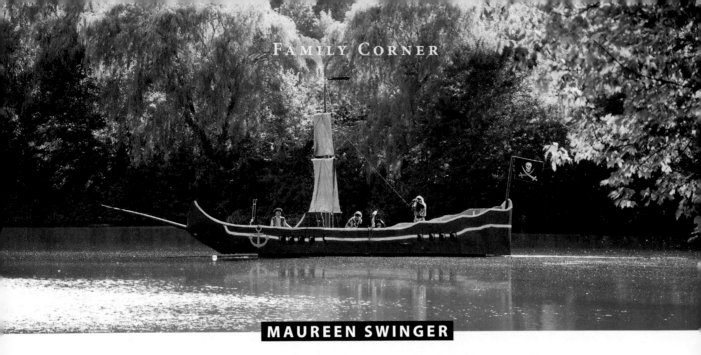

MAUREEN SWINGER

Buccaneer School

The children's dads built the cardboard-hulled ship in a week of late evenings.

ANY CHILD living in a Bruderhof community waits with uncontainable excitement for the opening day of first grade. In a nod to the community's beginnings, we continue an old German tradition of presenting each new first grader with a personalized *Zuckertüte* filled with candy and school supplies. Originally "sugar cones," these decorated paper *Tüten* are almost as large as the children themselves. But the best thing about the *Tüten* is the adventure kids must undertake to get them.

For weeks before the great day, the students' fathers have been scheming up some dramatic action to test the mettle of their sons and daughters. They conspire in secret, stealing away at odd hours to build magical contraptions and prepare the scene by the light of the moon. From wizards to Wild West shows, the theme is always a surprise. One year they made an enormous machine inspired by Dr. Seuss's Sneetches that input kindergarteners and output first graders.

The year my son joined the first grade, his class was just four boys. If any of them slept in the week preceding the ceremony, I was not aware of it. On the fateful morning, the entire community convened on the lakeshore, but no magic machines or cowboys appeared. There was nothing in front of us but tranquility – and antsy boys. Until –

A swell of majestic movie music heralded twin booms as two water-balloon cannonballs soared out into the lake. From a hidden, misty cove sailed a forty-foot ship with the Jolly Roger flying behind billowing black sails. The ship swung far out into the lake, then turned its bow straight at the crowd and sailed for port.

Amid piratical shouting, a large anchor was thrown out. Alas, it floated. A plank shot onto the bank and Long John Silver and Smee lurched out. They sang a rude song about Captain Hook, that rascally crook . . . until Hook himself came roaring down the gangplank, mustachio bristling

Maureen Swinger is an editor at Plough. *She lives at the Fox Hill Bruderhof in Walden, New York.*

with rage. He whipped his crew into shape, calling up four young new recruits to hunt for treasure. But first, they had to walk the plank: *onto* the deck, fortunately, not off. Smee was supposed to demonstrate, but halfway across, he lurched wildly and splatted in the muddy water. (I was not surprised. Smee is my husband.) After dumping out his boots and patching up his wounded dignity, he challenged the younger set to try.

With a right good will, the little guys boarded the ship, slurped some grog, and added their names to the rolls in blood-red marker. Having sold their souls to piracy, they grabbed their shovels and followed the treasure map to where X marked the spot – an innocent patch of grass. There they unearthed an enormous padlocked chest. But avast! The chest was empty. Where were their precious *Zuckertüten*?

Suddenly, from a muddy estuary, a flatboat shot onto the lake. Blackbeard the Terrible and his henchman gloated over a crate of stolen treasure. "Ha ha!" roared Blackbeard, "the *Zuckertüten* are mine! You will never go to school!"

The chase was on. Pirates big and small piled onto the ship, the seasoned hands fitting the new recruits with life jackets as they went. The cannons fired, the battle raged, and fate hung in the balance. Finally Blackbeard, bellowing on the stern of his boat, was felled by a water balloon and reeled backwards into the murk, followed by his henchman. They

fecklessly shouted and shook their fists as the triumphant Jolly Roger reclaimed its prize.

On the victory lap, the cannon boomed once more, but this time it fired a roll of toilet paper, which unfurled gracefully and fell in a long, wavering banner from sixty feet in the air. When the crew disembarked, the first-grade pirates sported tricorn hats and scimitars, looking so tremendously pleased with the success of their mission that their life jackets could hardly contain them. They stood at attention while Smee waded from ship to shore and presented them each with their long-awaited reward.

Happy sails, buccaneers; may the tides of school run fair. ⤳

Ahoy! View the piratical slideshow at plough.com/buccaneers.

New first graders with *Zuckertüten* in hand

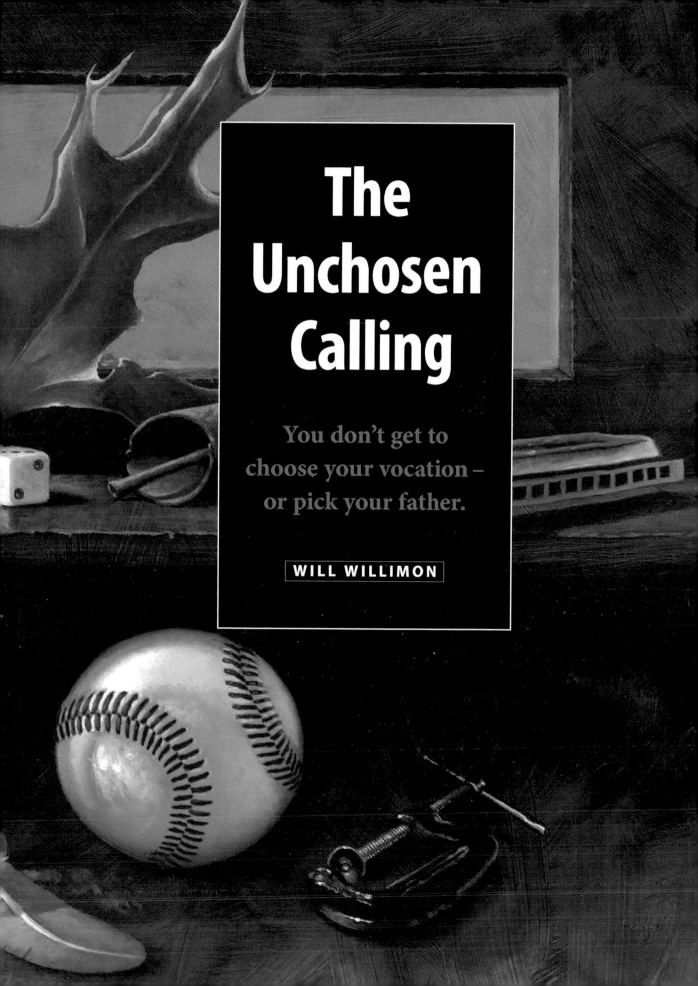

The Unchosen Calling

You don't get to
choose your vocation –
or pick your father.

WILL WILLIMON

All pencil sketches by the author

Artwork on previous spread: Timothy Jones, *Studio Curios*

AMONG THE IMPORTANT THINGS never mentioned at Sunday dinner conversations among the Willimons was the embarrassment of my father.

"What am I to say when they ask, 'Where's your father?'" I'd ask.

My mother's most detailed response: "Just say that your father doesn't live here anymore." *That's a relief. At least there was a time when I had a father.* I mined my memory for some shred of recollection. I remembered climbing into a man's lap and watching him fill his pipe with tobacco. There was also the scratch of whiskers. Then there was a memory of being in Skelton's grocery store with a man with a pipe who pulled a cold "dope" out of the cooler and handed it to me. When he did, someone in the store asked, "A Coakercoler for your grandson, right, Bob?"

The man who had given me the drink replied, "Go to hell. That's my *son!*"

Beyond that, nothing.

There was a tobacco humidor with pipes on the living room shelves. "Was that Daddy's?" I asked.

"Yes," was all I got. Sniffing the amber-colored jar provided my sole tangible confirmation of paternity.

One day, alone, rummaging in the desk I was forbidden to open, I found a letter from the warden of the US prison in Atlanta. "To whom it may concern: The prison record of Robert C. Willimon has been exemplary." *How would I live up to Daddy's success as a convict?*

As student body president of Hughes Junior High, I gave a speech one night to the PTA. The editor of the *Greenville News* came up afterward and said, "You've sure got that Willimon gift of gab. Who's your daddy, Charles or Gene?"

I gulped. "Robert was my father."

"No kidding? Didn't know Bob had a boy as young as you."

He bent down and whispered, "Bob could talk a preacher into breaking the Ten Commandments. That son of a bitch talked me out of ten thousand dollars. Left town. Never paid back a cent." *Another profession, banking, closed to me forever.*

"But I'll tell you this," he went on. "If your daddy walked right through that door and said, 'Bill, give me ten thousand dollars. I've got a great idea that'll make you rich,' I would whip out my checkbook. God-a-mighty, what a man with words!"

"I HEARD THE VOICE of the Lord, saying, Whom shall I send, and who will go for us? Then said I, Here am I; send me. And he said, Go, and tell this people . . . " (Isa. 6:8–9).

Methodists adore this passage. It's what the song "Here I Am, Lord" – written by Jesuit Dan Shutte in 1981, evolved to become a sort of Methodist national anthem – is based on. Few Methodists make it through two stanzas of this

Rev. Dr. William H. Willimon is a bishop in the United Methodist Church and professor of the practice of Christian ministry at Duke Divinity School. A former dean of the Chapel of Duke University, he is the author of many books, including Accidental Preacher: A Memoir *(Eerdmans, 2019), from which this article is adapted. Used by permission of the publisher.*

hymn without volunteering to go evangelize Zulus or at least to shed a maudlin tear. The chorus runs: "Here I am, Lord, is it I, Lord? I have heard you calling in the night. I will go, Lord, if you lead me . . . I . . ."

Note the prevalence of the first-person personal pronoun, as vocation degenerates into volunteering. Caught up in this syrupy tune, I wonder how many singers are truly challenged by the encounter with a summoning God. How many are actually willing to accept the risk

God who assigns us. To paraphrase Aquinas, we're contingent creatures. We're the moon, not the sun; our light is derivative, reflective of the Light of the World. The God who had the brilliant idea to breathe life into mud (Gen. 2:7) loans breath, but only for as long as God wills.

All sorts of lies keep us from knowing the truth of our contingency and dependency. The myth of self-invention underwrites the market that gives us fifty kinds of pizza and four hundred TV channels, and calls the resulting

Never have so many been so free to get so much of what they want yet have so little notion of the life worth wanting.

of being rescued from our overly cultivated subjectivity?

Vocation – called for by God – is a term scarcely used anymore. Vocation's power, said Hermann Hesse, is when "the soul is awakened . . . , so that instead of dreams and presentiments from within a summons comes from without," and an external relation "presents itself and makes its claim." The notion of an unchosen calling seems odd, schooled as we are in the fiction that our lives are our exclusive possessions to use as we choose.

"Who am I?" or "Why am I here?" evokes in unison the widely held individualist creed: I am self-fabricated, autonomous, my personal property, the sum of my astute choices and my heroic acts of detachment from anyone more important than me. I bow to no claim other than that to which I have freely consented. I'm the captain of my fate, master of my soul, author of the story that is me.

Christians assert the un-American conviction that our lives are less interesting than the

wasteland "freedom." Never have so many been so free to get so much of what they want yet have so little notion of the life worth wanting, making it impossible to choose themselves into the good life.

Augustine charged that our boasts of Promethean human freedom of choice are but the rattling of our chains, a failure truthfully to acknowledge our masters. In this supermarket of desire, endless, never really satisfied consumption is our fate. I tell myself that I am free of externally imposed masters while failing to admit my serfdom to the most imperious of lords: me.

Modernity compels us to write the story that defines who we are, heroically to choose from a variety of possible plots. Christians, on the other hand, believe that most of the important things that define us are accidental, externally imposed. The question is not "What do I want to do with me?" but rather "Which God am I worshiping and how is that God having his way with me?"

NOW WE COME to my discovery of the God who discovered me.

My sophomore dream trip to Europe (envisioned as a twenty-four-hour-a-day, three-month bacchanal) was commandeered by God and made a comedy of vocation. By midsummer 1966 a blue VW Beetle (purchased at the factory the Nazis built at Wolfsburg) deposited us in Amsterdam. In the Rijksmuseum, while my buddies explored the city that knows no sin, I stood face to

"Are you in Europe preaching?" I asked.

"I'm here to recover the Jew," he said, punching his finger into my chest. "Eight synagogues in five days. Rubbing my clean Christian nose in the ashes of the circumcised."

Very awkward pause.

"And you? Why are you here?" he demanded.

"Me? I'm just bumming around Europe with some guys, looking for girls, just having a good time."

I had awoken to an exam for which I had not studied.

face with the paintings I'd only seen as slides in Constance Armitage's Art History 101. I wondered before a melancholy Rembrandt self-portrait, so real I had to look away. To my right, an older man intently studied a van Ruisdael. He looked familiar, but who would I know so far from home?

Dr. Marney! A week or so of gray beard, but there he was – Carlyle Marney. Six months before, Marney (as he preferred to be called) had come to Wofford College's annual Religious Emphasis Week. He spoke with his deep voice that sounded like God, if Yahweh had been a Baptist from Tennessee. He swore, even in sermons, and made outrageous comments meant to thrill sophomores like me. I had retained none of his sermons' content, except something about Marney's horse in the pasture, turning its head when Marney whistled. Impenetrable metaphor for God?

I hesitantly approached. "Dr. Marney?"

"Who the hell are you?" he replied, looking me up and down cautiously.

"Oh, just a student at Wofford where you spoke last spring."

Marney stood there, assessing me.

"You take me for some kind of fool, boy? I've been a preacher long enough to know when somebody is lying."

"Uh, then I guess I don't know why I'm here," I stammered.

"Good! Maybe we can get somewhere. Unamuno says knowing that you don't know is the beginning of knowing. May I help?"

He grabbed my arm. "These Dutch have told me more truth than I can take in one afternoon. God, I need a drink. You?"

Marney led me down the steps, out the front door, and into the first bar outside the museum.

"Got bourbon?" he called to a waiter across the dim, smoky bar. "Doesn't need to be fine bourbon. This boy doesn't know the difference and I don't expect good mash this far from home. Two. Straight up."

Watching Marney fiddle with his pipe, I was excited, at last being taken somewhere dangerous.

"Now that you've got some liquor in you," he said after his first sip, "you ready to talk? No horseshit. Who brought you here? What's the reason you won't admit?"

Marney began tamping sweet-smelling tobacco into his pipe.

"Uh, I thought I was here just to see Europe. My first time and all. I really like art history . . ."

"You started this, barging in when I'm trying to come to terms with Abraham," mumbled Marney, accusingly, then settling back in his chair, closing his eyes as if he had heard nothing noteworthy.

"When you were speaking at Wofford, I got to thinking, or else I finally admitted to myself that I had been thinking, that maybe, I ought to think about applying for one of those Rockefeller grants for a trial year at seminary, but . . ."

Marney grinned as if he had finally figured me out. "Son, life's less monologue and more dialogue." I had awoken to an exam for which I had not studied.

"It's just I'm really bothered that I'd be thinking about seminary. It seems kinda crazy," I said nervously.

"Why crazy?" asked Marney, staring across the bar, feigning disinterest, puffing on his pipe.

I began a rambling narration. "I grew up without a father, you see. My father left us when . . ."

Marney shook his head. "No. Your daddy can abscond, die, disown, but everybody's got some daddy or another. I bet you went out and found one, didn't you? Besides, how the devil does not having a daddy explain you here, now? God's of the living, not the dead."

Timothy Jones, *The Quiet Muse*

I was grateful for the table between us. I blurted, "You see, since I've been at college I've gotten to read Freud, and I'm thinking, 'maybe my fixation on God is just my compensation for my lack of a father while I was growing up.' Wish fulfillment, maybe."

"Probably," smirked Marney.

"My thinking about God is just my psychological reaction to my daddy being in prison and all?"

"Look," said Marney, laying aside his pipe and moving toward me across the table as if to grab hold, aggravated at having to explain the obvious. "Son, God will use any handle God can get."

Timothy Jones, *Wood Box*

these?" he said, pointing to his empty glass. "My good man," he shouted to the waiter. "This round, don't spoil it with ice. My protégé likes it straight. *Garçon, encore bourbon!*"

Sometime before dawn, tossing, turning on the dirty mattress in the fleabag monastic cell that three of us had rented for eight dollars a night, accompanied by the sound of some student puking in the shared toilet down the hall, I said the words that Paul surely prayed when God blinded him: Why not somebody else? What kind of God would call somebody like me? But I don't want to be a Methodist preacher.

That night in Amsterdam was the birth of the accidental, initially humiliating, but eventually happy life that is not my own, summoned, made accountable to someone other than myself, answerable to an externally imposed claim. As Kurt Vonnegut used to say: "Keep your hat on; we may end up miles from here."

Too long a silence. Then I asked, "But, how can I figure out what's God and what's my own screwed-up background?"

In an exhale of smoke Marney pronounced, "Son, God will take advantage of any screwed-up background, crooked daddy, manipulative mama. Read the Scriptures, for God's sake! I swear, I've never known a preacher worth a damn who didn't have a bad mama or daddy problem. God can work with either. Be glad you only got one loss for God to take advantage of.

"Yep. I'm pretty sure God's got your name. Not the first time I've heard this story. You're nobody special. Got God's fingerprints all over it. You have time for me to have another one of

O**NE DAY IN HIGH SCHOOL,** I asked an aunt to violate family law and "tell me about Daddy."

Here's what she told me: When my older sister and brother were young, my father committed bank fraud, or bank robbery, or maybe both; it's hard to remember exactly. At the time, Daddy was reputed to have more liens against him for unpaid bills than anybody in the history of Greenville. His Greenville

Pickens Speedway, road construction company, and a dozen other brilliant ideas busted. He was sent to the federal pen in Atlanta, or maybe the one in Indiana, at one time or another; it's hard to remember.

Through it all, my mother stood by, awaiting his return. Daddy was released from jail and returned to the Willimon place. Nine months later, even though he and my mother were too unpleasant to lay upon a child. Their obfuscation produced a large void in my Eden.

I was twenty-two, at a family wedding in Raleigh, when my aunt Alice came into the motel room where we were gathered and asked, "Would you like to meet your father?"

"Yes, I guess."

Led into an adjoining room, I was greeted by an older man, smoking a pipe. We shook hands.

What a relief to know that God likes to make things; you can't devise yourself from scratch.

in their forties, I was born. Alas, my father's troubles resumed, and, after some misdeed that broke the proverbial camel's back, one Sunday the family had a meeting and decided it would be better for all if my father would leave.

Leave?

Mother was consulted and agreed, after being told that the family would look after me and my siblings (they were both more than a decade older than me). Daddy was written out of the will and my brother Bud, my sister Harriet, and I received the three-hundred-acre inheritance that would have gone to him. My mother's sole condition was that no one ever speak of my father because "this little boy ought not grow up with that burden."

Everyone kept that promise.

It's all absurd, of course, dark and sublime Faulknerian Southern Gothic worthy of Carson McCullers, Toni Morrison, or maybe even Eudora Welty. But people handled things differently back then. What was left of a family's fictional dignity must ruthlessly be preserved. Adults, having made a mess of so much, prided themselves in their ability not to mention a few things that were deemed

All I saw was an aging relative for whom I had no more feeling than for a distant cousin.

"I hear you have done right well for yourself," he said with a twinkle in his eye. "Hear you know how to make a dollar." *I have heard you are good at talking people out of money! Son, you make me proud.*

In my first church in Clinton, South Carolina, I paid a pastoral visit to Miss Agnes, who had been my mother's roommate at Winthrop College. "Willie, it seems like only yesterday that you were born!" she said after serving iced tea. "I remember visiting Ruby when she was expecting you. A terrible year, that was. She didn't care if she lived or died. Hair turned snow white during those nine months."

My nativity a "terrible year"?

"You can't expect her to have been happy about it. A forty-year-old woman surprised by a baby," she said with a dismissive little laugh as she offered me a cookie. "Still, I understand that you have brought her happiness. That's nice."

There you have it: I, the accident, the firstfruits post-prison.

Timothy Jones, *Tradition*

my biblical interpretation. Saint Paul did jail time, so did our Lord.

You can learn Greek, but if your old man hasn't been a convict, I brag to seminarians, vast portions of the New Testament will be incomprehensible.

"**I**T IS GOD that hath made us, and not we ourselves" (Ps. 100:3). Another shiny quarter memorization verse in Sunday school. What a relief to know that God likes to make things; you can't devise yourself from scratch.

That we are not self-made implies that we are God's property, to be called for as God pleases. As John Alexander points out in his 2012 book *Being Church*, in the New Testament the terms *calling* or *vocation* refer to discipleship

That's why I'm uneasy with the term "planned parenthood" and thank God that abortion wasn't readily available in 1946. God be praised for Bible stories of embarrassing pregnancies from Sarah and Hagar to Mary.

If I could have mustered resentment against my father, or the family who cast him out, or their vast conspiracy of silence, I could have tested my obedience to Jesus's command to forgive enemies. I could be the courageous victim who clenched his fist and overcame all. Alas, my lack of attachment to my unknown father produced too little antipathy for me to get over. I do believe that my father improved

rather than employment. We can be called to "eternal life" (1 Tim. 6:12) or into fellowship with Christ (1 Cor. 1:9), out of darkness into light (1 Pet. 2:9), and into right relationship with God (Rom. 8:30), but not to a career. Paul was a tentmaker (Acts 18:3), but nowhere is Paul "called" to be a tentmaker. Tentmaking put bread on the table, justification enough for Paul to give it his best.

Humans have careers; vocation is what God does.

The "mythologist" Joseph Campbell famously defines vocation as "following your bliss"; the theologian Frederick Buechner similarly says vocation is "where your deep gladness and the world's deep hunger meet." But bliss is made suspect by Jesus Christ – who casts fire on the earth (Luke 12:49), turning father against son (Luke 12:53), bringing not peace but a sword (Matt. 10:34). Jesus brings enlistment, incendiary vocation in mission that sometimes destroys bliss. Ask Paul.

"I like working with people, therefore . . ." or "I'm good with words, so naturally . . ." is not the way of vocation. How about nursing sick

of the ego. As Jesus succinctly says, "Ye have not chosen me, but I have chosen you, and ordained you, that ye should go and bring forth fruit" (John 15:16).

My adolescent, long-night-in-Amsterdam question, "What kind of God would choose someone like me?" is answered by Scripture. The God who chose Israel and the church chooses the likes of me.

God's got some form of discipleship in mind for everybody. Everyone can expect voca-

---

Vocation is not evoked by your bundle of need and desire. Vocation is what God wants from you.

---

people? No? That doesn't appeal? Hey, what about advertising?

Vocation is not evoked by your bundle of need and desire. Vocation is what God wants from you whereby your life is transformed into a consequence of God's redemption of the world. Look no further than Jesus's disciples – remarkably mediocre, untalented, lackluster yokels – to see that innate talent or inner yearning has less to do with vocation than God's thing for redeeming lives by assigning us something to do for God.

Without a Christ who summons, the sweet voice within is the best we can muster. But who, intently listening to his or her own subjectivity, risks anything as costly and crazy as God routinely demands?

"Mary, how did you decide, by listening to your life, to become pregnant out of wedlock, have a sword pierce your soul, and bear the crucified Son of God into the world?"

See what I mean?

Vocation is not an inner inclination awaiting discovery by rooting around in the recesses

tion – that peculiar way God uses you, creation of God, in God's salvation of the world. One of the happiest aspects of my happy pastoral life is watching the ways in which God calls – to write letters to the incarcerated, to do time on the church finance committee, to empty the bedpans of those in need, to raise a couple of godly children, to set a good table for the hungry, or to be a public school teacher.

At the Northside UMC Wednesday morning prayer breakfast (God and a sausage biscuit at an ungodly hour), I piously asked the assembled laity, "Pray for Mary. Johnny was booked last night. DUI. I'm going to see what I can do to get him out. Mary's had a time with that boy."

"How much you know about alcoholism?" said one of the men, unimpressed by my pastoral care.

"Where you going to get the money for bail?" asked another. "We'll go with you. Take this off the prayer list. We can handle it."

The three of us walked into the bowels of the jail, where we saw a frightened youth, huddled in the corner of a cell, weeping.

"Son, how long have you had a problem with alcohol?" one of the men asked through the bars.

"Uh, I wouldn't say I have 'a problem,'" Johnny replied.

"Let me rephrase that. How long have you been lying about your problem? Son, I've learned a lot about booze the hard way. Had that monkey on my back since I was in the army. I can show you the way out."

The father I barely knew selected that night – my biggest night at my new church – for his exit, this time leaving for good. As we drove to church that night, I was ashamed of my lack of response. Though I tried to lament the tragedy of it all, my grief was no greater than that I'd have felt for a distant relative. We hurried into church. I put on my robe, pulled tight the cincture, directed the candles to be lit, and formed the choir for the introit – "O Come,

You pull tight the cincture and pray, "God, who got me into this, give me the hardheaded determination to get through it."

"We're springing you," said another, who was a lawyer. "And you come home with me. Our kids are out of the house. Your mama's got enough on her already. I'd love to have somebody to watch Clemson football with."

A vocative God showing off.

It WAS CHRISTMAS EVE 1981. Northside United Methodist Church had a rough ride the years prior to my arrival as their new pastor. Things were so bad they found neither the funds nor the enthusiasm even for a Christmas service the previous year. The dispirited congregation needed a win. Even if I singlehandedly had to mold the candles, grow the poinsettias, and falsetto-croon "O Holy Night," by God my first Northside Christmas would be a candlelight extravaganza of Yuletide emotion.

As I was putting the finishing touches on my sermon for that night's service, my brother called.

"Daddy just died."

All Ye Faithful" instead of my preference, "In the Bleak Midwinter."

That's church for you. Church forces us to march in and sing even when we're not in a singing mood, not feeling faithful, and "joyful and triumphant" is not us. Church doesn't wait for you to have the proper motivation for worship in order to call you to worship. And there are so many times, when you have been called to be a pastor, that you don't feel like being a pastor but still must act the part. You may be in pain, may be in over your head emotionally and theologically. Though you are supposed to be an expert in helping others to grieve, you may not know how publicly to mark your own loss. As a pastor, your personal problems take a backseat to the needs of others. You're the only pastor they have, and Christmas comes but once a year. So you pull tight the cincture and pray, "God, who got me into this, give me the hardheaded determination to get through it." You go out and act like their pastor even when you don't want to.

That Christmas Eve at sad Northside, as at many other times and churches, I practiced the art of pastoral repression in service to my vocation. I stood up and played the preacher. Don't accuse me of deceit or denial – that night I was almost grateful for having something to pray over other than myself, pleased that baptism had given me a church family more messed up than my own, glad that a pregnant virgin is more newsworthy than a son unable properly to grieve the death of a failure at fatherhood.

I wasn't a hapless victim of poorly thought-out paternity. I was privileged to have been called for, compelled by my vocation to suck it up, take a deep breath, and stand and deliver, lay some Bible verse on them that would help them make it through the night. There was only me to say the divine words they couldn't say to themselves. Somebody's got to deliver the news, the good news for all who dwell in the land of darkness, whether it be east of Eden or on the north side of Greenville. Even though we "love darkness rather than light" (John 3:19), God incarnates anyway: *And the Word became flesh and dwelt among us . . .*

In each of our histories, there is regret and unfinished business. The world, as good as it is, is never enough. Not enough time, not enough room for complete redemption or full reparation. Even God Almighty shares one limitation with us finite humans, said Aquinas: Even God cannot make our past not to have been. No retrieving the lost days, no recalling just the right Bible verse to make the fix, no taking back the thoughtless word.

You can't. That's when you give thanks that the Word, the eternal Logos, became flesh, our flesh, and moved in with us. God refused to stay spiritual. The Word intrudes with words we cannot say to ourselves, Light shines in our darkness. God so loved the world in all of its screwedupness and regret. There's only us to tell the story. We step forward, anyhow. We sing. *O come, all you faithful.* Come on, all you unfaithful. Let's adore him anyway.

And wonder above wonders, in a dejected little church that nobody has heard of on ironically named Summit Drive in Greenville, damn South Carolina, with an emotionally inept preacher without even the grace to mourn his departed thief of a father, *God with Us.* Alpha and Omega enters our finitude, incarnating into our misspent histories.

An odd birth, an absent father, God come to those of unclean lips who could not come to God. Go ahead, Lord, live dangerously: send me. ⤳

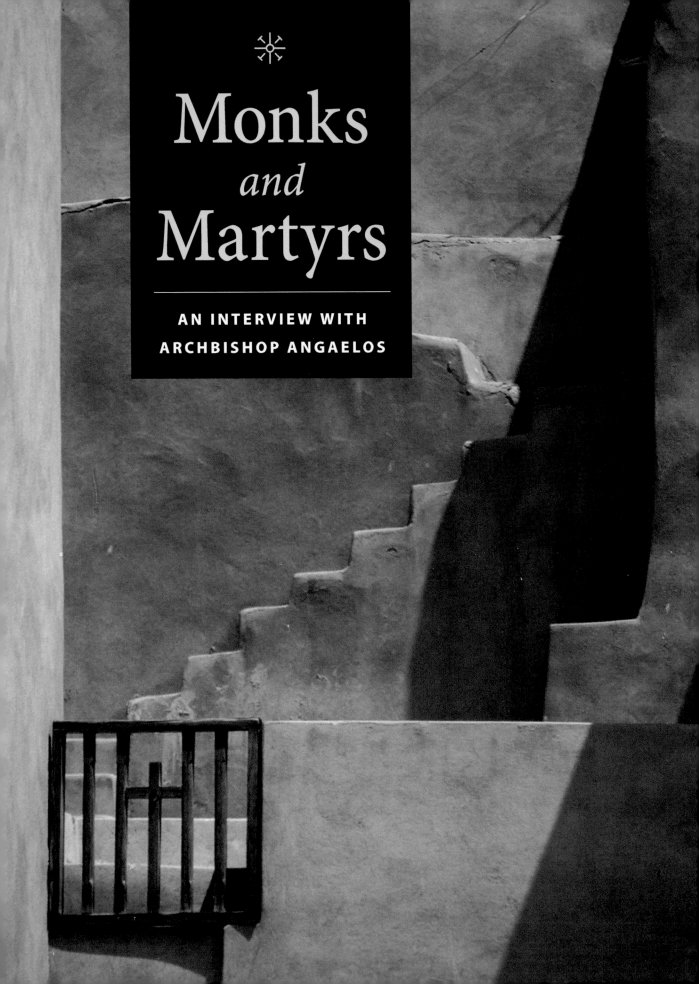

Monks
and
Martyrs

AN INTERVIEW WITH
ARCHBISHOP ANGAELOS

What can martyrs teach us about vocation? Archbishop Angaelos, the Coptic Orthodox Archbishop of London, speaks with _Plough_'s Peter Mommsen about the persecuted church today.

Plough: "Walk worthy of the vocation wherewith ye are called," wrote the apostle Paul (Eph. 4:1). What is this vocation?

Archbishop Angaelos: We all have a vocation: to be the "light of the world" and the "salt of the earth"; to be contributing members of our communities and of the Body of Christ. God gives us gifts so that we can use them as the faithful stewards did in the twenty-fifth chapter of Matthew's Gospel when they came and presented their Lord with the profits of what they had been given. To faithfully follow God is a vocation.

Of course, vocation can also more specifically mean calling to Christian ministry. That might be the offices of bishop, priest, and deacon, or it might be those who teach in Sunday schools, those who feed the homeless, or those who do other kinds of outreach.

There is also the calling, as was mine, to be a monk. Monasticism was established in the fourth century by Saint Anthony in the deserts of Egypt, and it is one of the pillars of the Coptic Orthodox Church. Today, we have vibrant monasteries and convents, where committed men and women follow their special vocation of praying for the church, praying for the world, and obeying the call to "leave all to be with the One." But they do not abandon the rest of the church, or the world: they serve the church and the world through their prayers. Our parish priests, on the other hand, are ordained as married men, while our monks and bishops are all celibate.

You yourself lived in a monastery. What brought you there?

I was born in Egypt. We migrated as a family to Australia when I was five. When I was a young man, I felt a strong calling to return to Egypt and join a monastery. I left Australia in 1990, when I was twenty-two, and, taking my lifetime vows of chastity, poverty, and obedience, joined the Monastery of Saint Bishoy, in the Valley of Scetis – Wadi El-Natrun in Arabic, which is halfway between Cairo and Alexandria, on the desert highway. This monastery was established in the fourth century, and some of the buildings actually date back to then. It is now home to about two hundred and fifty monks.

The decision to take lifelong vows to a religious community strikes many people today as a radical step. What led you to become a monk?

God speaks to us in the way he chooses. As you and I consider our callings, we can remember how it seemed at the time, and then we can perhaps see more, in hindsight. At the time, I felt moved to leave the world and go to the monastery. I had been very involved in my community in Australia – I served in the church, I had studied political science and philosophy, and then gone on to postgraduate study in law; I was working. But I left all that behind because I wanted to be in the wilderness to pray.

While the vast majority of monks remain in their monasteries for life, sometimes we are sent elsewhere. As I said, our parish priests are usually ordained as married men, but there are exceptions – as in my case. After a time in the monastery, I was sent to England to serve as a monk-priest in a very small parish. Then, I was consecrated as bishop, and now appointed archbishop.

The Monastery of Saint Bishoy, Wadi El-Natrun, Egypt

Photograph by Meilinda Goodwin/Bruderhof

Archbishop Angaelos with Bruderhof elder Paul Winter *(left)* at an event remembering the twenty-one Coptic martyrs, February 2019.

How do you account for the vibrancy of the Coptic monasteries?

We fast, we pray. Those ascetic practices that came out of the fourth century continue to be a crucial part of who we are. The monasteries are also a haven where, even in the midst of the strongest pressure to abandon the faith, men and women can go and find the living Church, relying on God.

Despite the misunderstanding of some non-Orthodox historians, the early monks and nuns did not flee to the desert to avoid martyrdom, because the monasteries themselves were targets, subjected to attacks by the Berbers around them, who killed many of the monks and nuns for their Christian faith; but the monasteries remain standing, and have outlived that persecution.

The monasteries are not just for the Christians, not just for the Copts, and they never were. My monastery has a trap door at the very top of the arch that overlooks the main entrance to the monastery from a safe height. The monks had it built in so that they could lower food, water, and medication to the attacking marauders. This is the ideal of Christian stewardship and of Christian hospitality. We must look after our communities, but also we must look after the world, even those who consider themselves our enemies.

Asceticism plays a role in the life of the laity as well. You fast for about two-thirds of the year and have daily prayers. Do you think there's a link between that rhythm of life and the willingness of so many in your church to suffer for their faith, and especially to accept the particular calling of martyrdom?

The fasts and the liturgies become an intrinsic part of how one lives one's life. There is a connection between one's own personal life of prayer, and the very public witness of martyrdom, as when the twenty-one martyrs were killed in 2015 by ISIS. It is there that we see the beauty of the Church.

Some may consider Coptic Orthodoxy to be antiquated or irrelevant, but when we see those martyrs, who very naturally witnessed to their faith, even paying the ultimate price, we realize that the Coptic Church is alive, and that it nurtures its children in a particular way. Fidelity becomes a totally inseparable part of who they are, and God gives us the grace to overcome this pain, to resist the pressure to abandon faith.

Can you describe what's been going on in Egypt over the last few years?

Well . . . this is not a matter of the last few years. Saint Mark preached Christ in Egypt in the middle of the first century. The Church has been there ever since, and we have suffered one form of persecution or another since then, and this continues in our contemporary history, particularly since the 2011 uprising against then-President Mubarak – the so-called "Arab Spring" – where there was a temporary breakdown of law and order.

Since that time, we have seen pockets of violent Islamism that have targeted Christians. Just in the past two years, we have lost about one hundred and fifty children, women, and men to acts of terrorism in the form of church bombings, shootings, and the targeting of Christian families and individuals, which has been ongoing in some regions. There were bombings of churches in Alexandria and Tanta on Palm Sunday, in the midst of celebrations; the shootings of the faithful leaving churches; and the shooting of pilgrims on a bus going on a pilgrimage to a monastery at least twice – one of these targeted a whole extended family returning from a baptism at a monastery.

The witness of the Coptic Christians in Egypt is that they continue to live their lives, even when they know that they are targets. I have known families that pray together before going to church, because they know that they may not all be coming back.

Pope Francis has used the phrase "the ecumenism of blood." How has the persecution of the Coptic Church in the last years opened new doors to Christian unity?

I first heard that expression from Pope Francis in Rome in 2013 at the fortieth anniversary of the signing of the Christological Agreement between our two Churches, settling the theological issue that had divided us in the fifth century.

We must remember that one of the twenty-one Libya martyrs of 2015 was not a Copt – he was Ghanaian. But persecution has a strange way of uniting us. When the persecutors come, they do not ask what denomination you are, they just kill you because you are a Christian. We share that designation by our persecutors, so surely, as the body of Christ, we should recognize that commonality.

Persecution does not affect Copts alone. Recently we have seen churches bombed in Sri Lanka and in Iraq; Christians have also been killed in Syria and in Nigeria. We must all take this personally; we must learn to pray for one another, to advocate for one another, and to share in each other's pain and joy. I cannot sit back and be comfortable with the fact that another human has been persecuted, and that is even more applicable when the other is a member, with me, of the body of Christ.

This past year, you and I have been at a number of events together to commemorate the twenty-one

martyrs. Theologically and culturally, it's hard to imagine a greater distance within the Body of Christ than that between my Anabaptist community, the Bruderhof, and the Coptic Orthodox Church. But it was striking to me how clear it was that we are one body. For example, in the Anabaptist tradition, too, there is a strong tradition of telling the stories of the martyrs. This does not do away with difference, but it certainly seemed to me to put it in the right place.

Absolutely. We should never gloss over theological difference, but it does not mean that we would not stand shoulder to shoulder in our work together, as the Coptic Church and the Bruderhof have done this past year.

We've talked about persecution, yet there's also a pressure that's less dramatic but possibly just as dangerous to our faith. Our liberated culture

The Monastery of Saint Bishoy, founded in the fourth century, is now home to two hundred and fifty monks.

The Syrian Monastery, Wadi El-Natrun, Egypt

prizes autonomy. We're supposed to always keep our options open. Discipleship, by contrast, is a calling that we don't choose. We can say yes or no to it, but we don't define what it is. And when we accept that call, when we give our full allegiance to Christ, we do not keep our options open. Is accepting the calling of discipleship more difficult today than in previous centuries?

Every era has its own challenges. Still, when I was sent out by His Holiness the late Pope Shenouda III to serve in England, he said something that has stuck with me. He said that the problem in the past had always been that there has been a choice between right and wrong, and people chose what is wrong. Whereas now, there is a blurring between what is right and what is wrong. That is what creates the challenge for our children, and for others we are trying to reach. Everything is now seen as relative. For some, there is literally nothing that should be considered sacred.

If we serve our children from a young age, if we guide them, if we show them that we ourselves are faithful and not hypocritical, then we will pass on the faith. If, in my preaching and in my conduct the message of Christ remains strong and clear, I will still be able to reach people. The Spirit within them will still be yearning for it.

Many Christians in the West seem to be in mourning for the days when Christianity dictated the boundaries of culture. Unlike the church in the West, the Coptic Church has been a minority religion for centuries. What might the experiences of the Coptic Church teach the Western church?

We are certainly a numeric minority in Egypt, as there are fewer Coptic Christians in Egypt than there are Muslims, but we reject being classified as a minority. For us in Egypt, as well as for the many Christian communities across the Middle East, we are the indigenous peoples of the countries that we still inhabit. We are natives.

Ninety percent of Coptic Christians are still in Egypt. Of course, that is a very different scenario than for Christians in Syria, or Iraq, Libya, and the Palestinian territories, where the vast majority of Christians have now left their homelands.

When one is placed under pressure, the way one lives one's faith changes. There is less opportunity for people to become indifferent, and so their witness is more existential, and more powerful.

You're a bishop – that means you're a shepherd. What does it mean to have that calling?

That calling always takes priority; I am committed to being available to the people who are in my care, for whom I am responsible. That is what keeps me going.

The relationships I have with these people to whom I have ministered over the past thirty years will always have priority. These are people who rely on me and with whom I have been entrusted. In our Church we have a very strong sense of direct pastoral ministry, where the priest or bishop is a father. Not *like* a father, but *actually* a spiritual father. This means that we do not retire, but we die in our ministry. When a bishop is enthroned to a diocese, as I have been, he serves it for his lifetime.

Because I started here in London as a priest, everybody in our congregations deals with me directly. While my office deals with all the outward-facing work, including all of our ecumenical relations, advocacy work, and so on, anything pastoral comes to me directly. People call me directly, and make pastoral appointments with me directly. I still do home visits, I still hear confessions. I am baptizing the children of the children I baptized when I first came. That stability is important for those we serve.

We are entrusted by God to serve his children, and it makes a difference whether we are faithful to that calling or not. The more faithfully we shepherd, the more people are able to really follow Christ in their lives and reach his kingdom.

We've been speaking of vocation. But there are people who feel they have no gift to offer – that they have no calling. How do you encourage them?

Well, firstly I would tell them that they are wrong. Everybody is given gifts. Our God is a generous God. He loves us as his children, and gives us gifts that we do not deserve and have not actually earned, so that we may use them for his kingdom. If we are not able to see those gifts, then either we have not been empowered by those around us to see them sufficiently, or we are giving in to a ploy of Satan to make us feel that we are of no value, and thus to render us ineffective. We all certainly have something to offer, but sometimes we cannot see it ourselves.

If we want to make an investment, we get a financial advisor. If we want to get fit, we have a fitness instructor. Likewise, when it comes to our spirituality, we need to have someone who guides us in discipleship. These are the people who will help us to find what our calling is, what our gifts are, and how to use them well. These are the people who will call us to account if we are not using them, or not using them properly. Our families, our faithful friends, our spiritual directors, our priests can certainly help us.

We always have something to offer, even if it is the widow's two mites or the young boy's five loaves and two fish. We are called, and that means that we are responsible before God to answer that call, and to use those gifts. Even if they look like they are of no consequence, that is false, and God is able to do so much more with them by the blessing that he puts upon them. ⤜

This interview from July 31, 2019, has been edited for clarity and length.

RACHEL PIEH JONES

A Love Stronger than Fear

Amid a volatile mix of disease, war, and religious extremism
in the Horn of Africa, what difference could one woman
make? Annalena Tonelli stayed anyway—and found a way
to beat history's deadliest disease.

IBRAHIM, a three-year-old Somali boy, suffered from both malnutrition and spinal tuberculosis. Policemen had found him in the desert in northeastern Kenya, dying of hunger. He clung to anyone willing to hold him and pressed his head against that person's chest. Annalena Tonelli, an Italian working as a teacher in Wajir, Kenya, took him home from the hospital; she wanted to keep him close through the nights too, so he wouldn't die alone.

When Annalena first stretched Ibrahim out on a bed, he pulled her down to lie beside him and rested his head over her heart. "Who knows how much he has suffered. Now he just wants comfort, peace, and the security of a mother's heartbeat," she remarked to another caregiver.

Life was harsh in the 1970s in Wajir, a remote region populated primarily by Somalis. A UNICEF survey declared the water unfit for human consumption. Lions attacked isolated nomads and snakebites were common. Temperatures soared to 105 degrees Fahrenheit and there was no electricity. Rain, on the rare occasions when it did fall, could lead to catastrophic flooding. The hospital lacked sufficient staff, equipment, and supplies. Tuberculosis, malaria, typhoid, cholera, and dengue fever raged.

Annalena moved to Wajir in 1970 to teach, but during a cholera epidemic her work shifted to caring for sick children like Ibrahim. Eventually, she turned all her attention to treating tuberculosis, an infectious disease that carried a powerful stigma among Somalis (and still does). People wouldn't use the word tuberculosis and insisted they only had a cough. If a community found out a member had TB, the sick person was often ostracized or even abandoned. Many would rather die than be labeled with the diagnosis.

In the developed world, many still assume that TB no longer exists. Dr. Paul Farmer, who battled TB in Haiti, put it bluntly: "The 'forgotten plague' was forgotten because it ceased to bother the wealthy." That only began to change in 2016 when cases increased in the United States for the first time in decades, and in the following year, when drug-resistant TB started killing people in Minnesota. Around the same time, South Korea announced new laws requiring that every citizen be tested twice in his or her lifetime. Media reports contained elements of shock that this Victorian-era disease was still among us.

Dr. Onkar Sahota, chair of London's Health Committee, said in 2015, "We think TB is a disease of developing countries or of days gone by, but TB is a disease of today. It certainly was a disease of yesterday and we need to make sure it isn't a disease of tomorrow."

ANNALENA HADN'T KNOWN much about tuberculosis when she moved to Kenya, but since her youth she had been drawn to the sick, the poor, and the outcast. In her hometown of Forlí, Italy, she had founded an organization called the Committee to Fight World Hunger. But to her, that hadn't been enough. She discovered a slum known as Casermone, and started spending more and more time there. She took children from Casermone to medical appointments, paid school fees, and even clipped their toenails. The phone at her house would ring, someone would demand wood or coal, and off Annalena would rush.

Rachel Pieh Jones writes from Djibouti, where she and her husband run an international school. In October Plough *will publish her book* Stronger than Death: How Annalena Tonelli Defied Terror and Tuberculosis in the Horn of Africa, *from which this article is adapted.* plough.com/StrongerThanDeath

She urged her friends and siblings to join her and they would, drawn in by her persuasive charisma. One friend, Maria Teresa, became Annalena's lifelong partner in her vision to serve. When later asked what inspired Annalena, who was raised Catholic and had a deep love for Jesus, Maria Teresa said, "Gandhi, Gandhi, Gandhi." She added, "She learned from Gandhi that to love one must willingly and deliberately strip away self and restrict one's own needs." Annalena referred to the Indian independence leader as her "second gospel."

During the early 1960s, while Annalena was reading Gandhi, there were also radical shifts in Italian Catholicism. The Second Vatican Council encouraged dialogue with other religions and challenged lay people to live out missionary vocations both locally and globally. Believers wouldn't have to become nuns or priests, or even work under the auspices of the church, to serve the poor or play a meaningful role in the spiritual life of their communities. This suited Annalena's independent streak, as did the renewed emphasis on social action as a valid form of the vocation to mission. Her experiences in Casermone led her to search for a place where she could live and serve among the poor for the rest of her life. Inspired by a friend, Pina Ziani, who worked among lepers in east Africa, Annalena settled on Kenya. Pina helped her secure a teaching contract and Annalena left Italy in 1969.

"The poor are waiting for us," Annalena said in one of her few public statements. "The ways of service are infinite and left to the imagination. Let us not wait to be instructed in how to serve. We invent and we live the new heavens and the new earth each day of our lives. . . . If we don't love, God remains without an epiphany. We are the visible sign of his presence and we make him alive in this infernal world where it seems that he is not. We make him alive each time we stop next to a wounded person."

ONCE IN KENYA, Annalena became independent from the limitations and structures of the Catholic Church. Yet she knew she needed a supportive community around her. Soon Maria Teresa and five other women had joined her. They prayed and read scripture together in the mornings and spent their days caring for the sick. They built a physiotherapy facility and called it the Farah Center, or Center of Joy.

Maria Teresa and the other women provided therapy for those with disabilities caused by polio and other childhood diseases. Annalena was consistently drawn to the poorest and most outcast. At that time, due to the lack of medical care, superstitions, and stigma, this meant her focus turned to Somali nomads with tuberculosis.

One young woman, her name lost to sand and history, was typical of those she served. The woman had suffered polio and now hovered near death from tuberculosis. Annalena sat by her side in the final hours of her life. Though they couldn't communicate in any shared spoken language, Annalena said she and this woman understood one another.

The woman's legs were limp, thin as sticks, her body so emaciated it was frightening – a rice sack filled with bones. But her face was filled with expression, an awareness. According to the dictates of her clan, she wore the black veil of a married woman, dignified in its modesty. Even though she was now divorced, she still bore the pride of a woman who had been married, once chosen.

She asked Annalena, with hand gestures and her eyes, to spend the coming night in the room with her. The woman coughed incessantly. Annalena sat beside her. Here was one of "God's sparrows" – one of Annalena's favorite terms for describing the sick – falling to the ground, known by her Creator and neglected by her people.

Annalena grew drowsy, the heat pushing her head down toward her chest, urging her to sleep. She prayed to keep herself awake. The heat and fever weakened the sick woman. Annalena wrote that she "loved her with an infinite tenderness." Even that love couldn't keep Annalena's eyes open for the nightlong vigil.

When her head drooped and her body collapsed in sleep, the woman took the dirty pillow from behind her own head and offered it to Annalena. Annalena didn't refuse, though the pillow was full of infection.

Around five o'clock in the morning, Annalena woke, took the woman's hand, and smiled at her. "Maybe at the end of my life I can say that all I did was pass through this world, holding the hand of the dying, smiling tenderly," she said later. The light of the kerosene lamp illuminated the woman's face. She fought to speak. "God is . . . in the name of God, gracious, merciful . . . go!" And she died.

"These people must have an extraordinary reward in heaven," Annalena wrote, "because they have suffered so darkly on earth."

"The ways of service are infinite and left to the imagination. Let us not wait to be instructed in how to serve."

Annalena Tonelli

DESPITE THE INFECTED PILLOW and ongoing close contact with the sick, Annalena rarely got sick. Occasionally she battled malaria or exhaustion, but she never tested positive for tuberculosis. At Wajir's hospital, Annalena started to oversee TB medication. Friends in Italy sent her books and articles about TB control and combination therapy. She traveled to Spain, then London, to take medical courses. She learned about a recent experimental exploration of short-course therapy, which could theoretically cut the time of care from eighteen months to six. Given its 33 percent success rate, she felt, it shouldn't be difficult to do even a little better. Treatment was simple and straightforward but had to be followed with precision: patients had to take the right pills at the right time.

That, Annalena believed, was something she could make sure would happen.

The trouble was getting nomads to stay in one place long enough for the cure to take

Photograph by Eric Lafforgue on Flickr

Patients signed an agreement to stay at the center. In fact, they had to designate a relative who could chase them down if they left early.

hold. Eighteen months? Impossible. But six months? Maybe, just maybe, for a good reason, a nomad could be convinced to stay. But not in a hospital, beneath a roof, or inside the prison of four cement walls. Not without their animals or families. Not without some sense of autonomy, dignity, and productivity.

If the right context of care could be created, the right combination of medicine and relationship established, a nomad might stay. Annalena had been in Wajir long enough to know what Somalis valued most highly: Islam, community, and independence.

Her idea was to invite nomads to the property around the Farah Center, where they could build their huts on her land. They could bring some of their animals and a family member or two. She would have them sign an agreement that they would not leave until their six months of treatment were completed and their sputum test came back negative. She would oversee every single pill dosage and provide meals. She planned to build a mosque and a school. She

would create jobs for patients. Above all, she would know them: their names, their families, their stories. She would listen to their voices and hold their hands and kiss their cheeks, even while they exhaled tuberculosis bacteria. She would tend their wounds and their hearts.

Before Kenya could actively promote the new short-course treatment, the country needed to run a trial, to make sure patients were actually cured and that the treatment wouldn't contribute to drug resistance. In April 1976, Annalena proposed to the Kenyan Ministry of Health that she manage a tuberculosis control test project in Wajir. She received permission to launch her project, with funding from the World Health Organization and the United Nations High Commissioner for Refugees.

In naming her new project, Annalena was careful not to use the word tuberculosis – she never would in her centers. Instead she named it the Bismillah Manyatta, the Village in the Name of God.

The sick came with their camels and the canvasses, ropes, and bent sticks for building their huts. Soon dozens were scattered across the sand near the Farah Center. There was no real wall, so beyond a small row of trees and a welcome sign, huts expanded outward as more and more people were drawn to the village.

Each patient was started on the new short-course therapy. Somalis presented so sick and at such late stages of TB that their dosages had to be adjusted almost weekly as they gained weight from the therapy and the nutritious diet provided. Once the huts were built, people had slightly more motivation to stay put, but still Annalena had to enforce compliance. Patients signed an agreement to stay at the center; in fact, they had to designate a relative who could chase them down if they left early.

Beyond this one promise, Annalena put pressure for compliance on herself, rather than on the patient. Part of her task involved directly overseeing the administration of the medications, down to the actual ingestion and swallowing of them. Annalena kept meticulous records and direct observation became central to her treatment.

People lined up at a table where she set out their pills and small cups of water or the orange drink she despised as too sweet, and her stack of medical charts. One by one, they swallowed the medicine. If someone was too sick to come to the table, she visited their hut. Sometimes she placed the pill on their tongues. She managed these pills around the clock, on a four-hour rotation.

TB pills were large and hard to swallow. If someone refused, Annalena sat with them until they swallowed the medicine. If someone vomited, she brought a glass of water, sometimes a slice of cake to settle the stomach.

"I was with them every day," she said. "I served them on my knees. I was beside them when they were getting worse and did not have anybody to take care of them, to look them in the eyes, to give them strength." Over her thirty-four years in the Horn of Africa, Annalena would achieve a remarkable 93 percent cure rate.

She found the work was both invigorating and exhausting. A Muslim elder in Wajir donated land so Annalena could build a hermitage, a place of retreat where she could be spiritually rested and renewed. She dreamed of spending a year in the hermitage, but a backlog of work heaped up on her desk. She had so many guests at the Manyatta that she read her Bible and prayed at five o'clock in the morning to avoid interruption. New patients, old patients, hungry children, everyone wanted to see her or ask her for something. Maria Teresa called it a "lacerating dichotomy between silence and the sick. The poor called her back from the hermitage, back to their hell, but she knew it was God who took her to the poor and the poor who took her to God."

She tried to only go to the hermitage when she was sure no one was about to die. People who could sense death's nearness turned their beds to face Mecca, then called for Annalena. "They wanted one hand held by the sheikh and one hand held by Annalena," Maria Teresa told me. "The sheikh prayed the Koran and Annalena prayed silently, and together they accompanied the person to the door of eternity. So interesting, that a pure Muslim would want an infidel."

ANNALENA REMAINED in Wajir until 1985, when her role in exposing a massacre jeopardized her safety and ability to continue. The Kenyan government kicked her out and refused to renew her visa. She moved to Somalia, where she established more tuberculosis treatment centers. Again, she

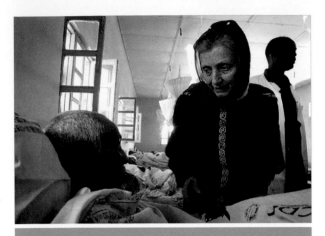

Photograph @ UNHCR/E. Parsons

> People who sensed death's nearness would turn their beds to face Mecca, then call for Annalena.

found herself caught up in violence, this time the civil war. She moved to the relatively stable and peaceful region of Somaliland, northern Somalia, and continued her work with the sick.

Most people loved her, but some grew resentful of her presence: a foreigner, a Christian, and a humanitarian whose work drew attention to the weaknesses of the medical care system and local prejudices. In 2003, Annalena won the prestigious Nansen Refugee Award, which increased her profile in Somalia and internationally.

On October 5, 2003, after three decades of serving Somalis with TB and AIDS, Annalena was gunned down by Islamic extremists as she made the evening rounds of her patients in the TB hospital she had founded in Borama, Somaliland.

I was living a few blocks away when Annalena was murdered, having moved to Somaliland in early 2003 with my husband and two children. My husband had taken a job at Amoud University in Borama. Though I never met Annalena, learning about her changed how I wanted to live my life.

THE HERMITAGE still stands in Wajir. It is a plain, simple structure; a patch of dirt surrounded by a wall, two small rooms, and a two-story tower with a terrace. Weeds have grown and scraps of garbage pile up in the corners. The Kenyan nuns who work in the Farah Center sometimes come here to pray, but not often. The iron rungs leading to the tower remain firmly implanted in the wall. Retracing Annalena's footsteps, I scramble up them and perch on the ledge, gazing out over Wajir.

When Annalena stood here, she saw an expanse of open desert and the occasional acacia tree. The town has grown since then and my view is hampered by houses and buildings. Minarets puncture the sky. Camels lumber over dirt trails through town, led by young herders with sticks slung over their shoulders. The wells once on the outskirts of Wajir are now in the center. Where marabou storks once stepped between camels and nomads at the watering holes, truckers use generators to pump water and wash their vehicles.

Behind me, across the dirt road, is the Bismillah Manyatta, still used to house and treat nomads with tuberculosis. Inside the hermitage, down below, is a well with an inscription, "My soul is thirsty for God, the God of my life." Here, in this place provided by a Muslim for use by Christians, surrounded by stark desert beauty and the vibrant life of a growing town, I feel the possibility of peace, of a world not torn asunder by hatred, fear, and isolationism. I understand why Annalena lingered here. ❧

Now and at the Hour

JOSEPH MICHAEL FINO

WHAT BUSINESS does a man have in a hospital room – in the brief moment at the end of a long life lived everywhere and with everyone else – holding a hand and loving every year of a life he knows nothing about? There have been so many rooms that when I imagine the fifth floor of Calvary Hospital each nameplate at each doorjamb rapidly morphs into the next. There is only one constant: a janitor in a green jumpsuit waxing the linoleum floor. He waxes widely, slowly, left to right then reverse, Eddie Vedder growling through his headphones.

These names, changing and changing, persist somehow within me unchanged. These faces find me. They surprise me, coming into focus without me even closing my eyes – staring out a car window into a leafless wood or at a clean slice of blueberry pie or at the Host. I have awoken at night with a name and a prayer on my lips – "pray for us now and at the hour of our death" – often wondering if, at this moment, the petition might be redundant. What joins a man to another he's known for so few hours at a time? Could it have something to do with that thoughtless-heartless monster, Cancer, pulverizing any hapless cell underskin? Alexander. Rose. Madelyn.

> **Pastoring souls through the valley of death is a work one carries out long after a corpse is bagged.**

~

Intimacy is not just for familiars at home. Death, at certain of her portals, can be intensely intimate.

~

Are you there? I catch myself wondering of a leaking, breathing corpus laid out on a hospital bed, eyes open and vacant. Life has its way of deceiving us. Sometimes the soul feels so loosely attached to a body, like a tooth you could tie a string around and – slam! – dislodge. Other times the soul feels so securely lodged in a patient that you expect heaven itself to descend and lift them both together behind its jeweled walls, into its duskless day. In either case it is the body, I like to think, that is steeped in soul, and it is Death who deceives if one thinks we can be finally ripped asunder.

It's strange, too, to insert yourself into a relationship – of spouses, say – at its most tender and delicate apex. "Married fifty-five years," a man said to me while looking over my shoulder – the way you might catch a new dad gaze longingly upon an incubated premie – at his wife. Every day at three he prayed the rosary from an upholstered chair at her bedside. The last time I saw her was early one afternoon. She woke from sleep to find me praying a chaplet. Too weak to talk, too gracious not to smile with just the wrinkles around her eyes. Loraine.

~

It's not that they haunt me, these names and faces; the word is too strong and with the wrong connotations. But the names don't go away, like leaves on the scrim of a rapid are submerged by the turmoil of currents, only to reemerge in a different bend of the river at a different hour.

Pastoring souls through the valley of death is a work one carries out long after a corpse is bagged, downed through the elevator shaft, and later downed more deeply into the earth, since, as we all seem to expect, a life goes on living this day and every day. Another name appears beside the door, but the flock doesn't diminish. Each remains at the pastor's side through the shadowed valley. They have

A member of the Franciscan Friars of the Renewal, Brother Joseph Michael Fino lives at St. Leopold Friary in Yonkers, New York.

become his own. Some you meet as "Kathleen," for example. But the prayers you offer *in memoriam* are for an Aunt Kath.

～

I was not prepared for the affection of families. I was not prepared for the silent communion one has with the incommunicative. The presence of another, as silent and unresponsive as it may be, is unique, always unrepeatable and mournable. I was not prepared for the angry: the woman whose skin lagged off her bones and whose voice came like a foghorn ("No! Arrrggg!!") whenever she saw me. I am ashamed to say I never learned her name.

I was not prepared for the agony. When I saw Deborah, she was in teeth-grinding torture. Each visit I found her sidelong, her fists clenched around the bars of the hospital bed, terror being worked out in her eyes. I would give her the Eucharist. She chewed Him, I thought at first, like one taking revenge, as if she could mortally masticate the living God. As I knelt at her side and watched her commune, I saw her eyes, wide and looking around, still working out that terror, and saw that her heart was not on vengeance. I was looking upon something I couldn't understand – like a child who walks in on adults reconciling.

～

I never felt very priestly at Calvary. The sacrifices were always offered by others, the sheep already in the teeth of wolves. Nor did God need me to make his visits. Marta: "Listen. I want to tell you something. I think God visited me. I woke up at night and he was there."

"How did you know he was there?"

"He was running his fingers through my hair. *It's going to be OK*, he said. That's just

Mary Pal, *Lighthouse Keeper*, cheesecloth on canvas, 2018

Mary Pal,
Looking Back,
cheesecloth
on buckram,
2013

what he said. *It's going to be OK.*"

"And do you believe him?"

She looked very serious when she replied, "Yes. I do." Then added, "I wanted to tell you because no one else would believe me. They would say it's the drugs or my sickness or that I'm getting old, losing my mind."

The first time I met Marta, she received a phone call from her sister just after I placed the Host in her mouth. She answered the phone and, in aggravated argument, managed to utter a couple expletives before swallowing. That was weeks earlier. The last time I ever saw her, she slept – cradled in the morphine drip, matted hair, thin as a rail – for the entire rosary I prayed from the armchair.

It impressed me how she received the word God spoke at her bedside. *It's going to be OK* wasn't negated by her imminent death. In her mind, there was no contradiction between word and event. The two were of a piece, sacramental. "He was running his fingers through my hair," she had said. The prophet Ezekiel records that the Lord "will rescue [his sheep] from all places where they have been scattered on a day of clouds and thick darkness." I wonder sometimes if that day of clouds and thick darkness might describe, not the day of scattering, but the day in which the sheep are finally rescued.

～

People die. That has been for me the least welcome aspect of this assignment. It's the kind of thing you foreknow, but foreknowledge is different than experiential knowledge. The former is abstracted. The latter, visceral.

Maggie lay in a persistent vegetative state. As I read to her the fourteenth chapter of John's Gospel, I found myself absorbed in her presence. The way a child absorbs himself in a brook which he looks upon from its grassy banks for the moveless movement of minnows. In the clean water, he might see them translucent and swimming still; he might see them, if he's patient, spurt upcreek like light.

There is a lot to life that we don't see, won't touch, until it touches us and pulls us into its depths. After greeting Guillermo, apparently incommunicative – a touch on the shoulder, a word spoken from my knees to his upward-staring face – I visited with his daughter and granddaughter. We all prayed together. Then, after taking Guillermo's hand to say goodbye, I was jolted by his stonemason grip and a groan which bore into me his deep gratitude. ～

The Language of Frailty

ANNE-SOPHIE CONSTANT

Jean Vanier, founder of the L'Arche community movement, died on May 7, 2019, at age ninety. In this excerpt from Plough's new biography, the renowned spiritual writer and champion of the weak finds that the core members of his community, those with severe physical and intellectual disabilities, still have much to teach him about himself.

I N 1980, Jean Vanier decided to resign from his position as director of the L'Arche community in Trosly in northern France and take a year's sabbatical. The following year, in November, he moved to La Forestière, a L'Arche house for people with severe disabilities that had opened in 1978. This had been a dream of his for a long time.

La Forestière, surrounded by the forest, as its name suggests, was a new, one-story building constructed around a bright central patio. It was flooded with light from the large bay windows that opened onto the garden. There was a fireplace in the large room where one could stop for a cup of coffee or for evening prayers. It had a small chapel

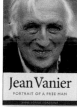

Anne-Sophie Constant lectured at the Conservatoire National des Arts et Métiers in Paris until 2012. A friend of Jean Vanier for decades, she is the author of Jean Vanier: Portrait of a Free Man *(Plough, August 2019).* plough.com/jeanvanier

with a very low altar that allowed a person with disabilities, stretched out on the knees of an assistant seated on the ground, to see what was happening. The atmosphere was peaceful. People here took their time; the community seemed to move in slow motion. This was a place where there was plenty of time to get close to one another, so that someone who is blind and deaf could touch a person who approaches. There was plenty of time to bathe Eric – a resident whose body was curled up by disability and despair – slowly unknotting his limbs, letting him feel the warm water, letting him play with the soap, washing him. There was plenty of time to feed Lucien, so that he might feel the pleasure of tasting, swallowing, and smelling the food. These broken bodies were touched with respect and tenderness. While someone gently wiped away the saliva dripping down Henriette's chin, someone else gently took hold of the hand of Loïc, who had just struck himself violently on the nose. They restrained him without harshness, respecting what he might have been trying to express by his actions, reassuring him that he had been heard, and he was not alone.

At La Forestière one must learn to understand the language of the body. It is a language of tenderness and frailty. The body, which is exalted in athletics and fashion and despised in sickness, aging, and disability – this same body is, the apostle Paul writes, a temple of the Holy Spirit. The broken body, then, is a broken temple that lets the light of God pass through more easily. Jean Vanier knows that the Gospel is the story of a God who chose to be born in human form, with all its brokenness and frailty:

The Word did not become flesh
in the same way one puts on a piece of clothing
only to discard it again;

A Difficult Love

JEAN VANIER

Near the end of his life, in an interview with the Anglican priest Nicky Gumbel, Jean Vanier recalled the genesis of L'Arche back in 1964.

PEOPLE WITH DISABILITIES are the most oppressed people of this world. I visited an institution where there were eighty men, completely locked up, no work. They were just sitting around with quite a lot of violence and screaming. And strangely enough, I was both attracted and repulsed.

When I left the Navy, I wanted to live in community *with* the poor, not *for* the poor. And so we lived together, and it was an extraordinary experience of joy. They were so happy to get out of that institution. We lived around the table – going to buy food, cooking your food, eating your food, doing the washing up, and then starting again. And somehow, at the heart of what we were living was the message of Jesus. In Luke, Jesus says, "When you give a meal, don't invite your family, your rich neighbors, your friends; when you give a *really* good meal, invite the poor, the lame, the blind and the rejected." And then he says, "And if you do that, you are blessed." It's one of the secret beatitudes of the gospel.

What happens when you sit to eat with people is that you become friends. Aristotle says, "To become a friend of someone you must

it is flesh becoming divine,
becoming the means by which that life of love
from God
in God
communicates itself.
That life is not an idea that can be learned
from books or teachers;
it is the presence of one person to another,
the total giving of oneself to another,
heart to heart,
in a communion
of love.

As Francis of Assisi's encounter with lepers allowed him to discover "a new softness in his body and spirit," La Forestière was a decisive new step in the life of Jean Vanier. For a year, he experienced the rhythm of life with these men and women with severe disabililties – the rhythm of Eric, for instance, a seventeen-year-old who was blind, deaf, and unable to walk or feed himself. Abandoned in a hospital at four years of age, he was so desperate for human contact that he clung with all the strength in his arms to anyone who passed close to him. Jean discovered that Eric reciprocated all the love he showed him. Jean washed, clothed, fed, and calmed him, reassuring him by these actions that he could be loved, and therefore that he was lovable. For his part, Eric introduced Jean to a new form of peace. Jean writes:

> At La Forestière, every evening after dinner, I put Eric in his pajamas, then we spent a half or three-quarters of an hour in prayer, all of us together in the living room, both the disabled people and the assistants. I often sat with Eric on my knees; he rested. And I discovered that I rested with him. I didn't feel like talking. I was at peace, with an inner quiet. He also was at peace; he also felt content. It was a moment of healing. I found inner harmony again.

eat a sack of salt together," which means many meals. We had such fun, but somewhere there was a sense that we were to be together in order to reveal the kingdom of God. The kingdom of God is a place where the poorest and the rejected come together to celebrate their joy, because they have discovered that they are loved by the people around them and they are loved by Jesus. It's an incredible joy, because they don't want power, they don't want to go up the ladder of more money, more success, more status – all they want is to be happy.

That's what people see as they come here. But inside you have the reality of complex relationships and all the rest. It's a place of the kingdom, but you have to work at it. What appears as something beautiful implies also difficulties; we have to work at it and discover that to love is not easy.

There is something very special as we approach those who only need love, which are people with disabilities. They don't need knowledge; they can't pass any exams. Some can't even speak. But they discover that they are loved. There's a closeness between the crying out of those who have been rejected and pushed down and humiliated – "Does anyone love me?" – and the revelation that God is love. It's a strange and beautiful meeting. ⇒

This interview transcript from 2017 has been excerpted and edited for clarity. Used with permission of Nicky Gumbel. Watch the full interview at plough.com/vanier-gumbel.

But those times when Eric clammed up, howling and writhing, when nothing could calm him down and he was overwhelmed by darkness, Jean Vanier found a door opened to hidden distress, violence, and fear buried in his own heart. He discovered a whole world of chaos and hate within himself that he had carefully masked with his education and intelligence or buried in his work and activities. Reflecting on such angst is a recurring theme in Jean's thought. He has realized that it is an inescapable part of the human condition. "Cows do not experience anguish," he jokes. Contained in a secret part of our being, this anguish can emerge suddenly, along with the violence it produces, at the least hurt. Jean says he still feels within himself today that "it is like a bomb ready to explode, driving us to call for help."

Discovering his own inner violence has allowed him to recognize similarities between himself and the intellectually disabled he cares for, similarities to which he had previously been blind. He feels as though he has been knocked off an invisible pedestal – his goodness – which is humiliating, but also liberating. "I have been brought face to face with my own deep reality, with my own truth. . . . I begin to be myself. I no longer play the great and powerful grownup, striving for first place, for success, and for admiration; I am no longer worried about appearances. I allow myself to be the child that I am, the child of God."

At La Forestière, then, it is no longer a question of Jean Vanier and Eric – the adult and the miserable child – but of "two children playing a game of the soul," a game which, the poet Pierre Emmanuel tells us, connects us to "the fields of eternity" where all springs of love find their superabundant source. Communion – that other word for love – allows us to be together in God, Love Himself, who unites and gathers us. Eric evokes this mystery of peace and union in anyone who comes close to him and takes time with him, because he does not ask for anything more, and does not try to control or dominate or use anyone.

In his relationship with Eric, Jean Vanier was finally able to understand this sentence from the Gospels that he had heard many times: "Whoever welcomes this little child in my name welcomes me; and whoever welcomes me welcomes the one who sent me. For it is the one who is least among you all who is the greatest." Jean reflected in a newsletter, "This is the mystery that is revealed to us in L'Arche today: the poorest person leads us directly to the heart of God. The smallest one heals our wounds, sometimes by painfully revealing them to us. And that healing and that experience of Jesus and his Father come through the heart-to-heart relationship of mutual trust that grows between us." ⮞

Icon and Mirror

A photo-essay on the women of Voronezh, Russia

POLA RADER

RUSSIAN ORTHODOX Christians often take a dim view of feminism. Despite advances in women's rights in Russia since women gained the right to vote in 1917, in the world of Orthodoxy women still play a clearly defined role.

Does this traditional view mean an infringement of women's rights? Can the voice of modern Orthodox women be heard in the church today? These questions were the starting point for my photography project "Icon and Mirror," in which I explore the relationship between the idealization of the iconic Virgin Mary, on the one hand, and the treatment of real women in today's Russia on the other.

A parishioner after the Sunday service. All photographs by the author.

Pola Rader is a conceptual documentary photographer and filmmaker based in Kiel, Germany. More of her work can be found at polarader.com.

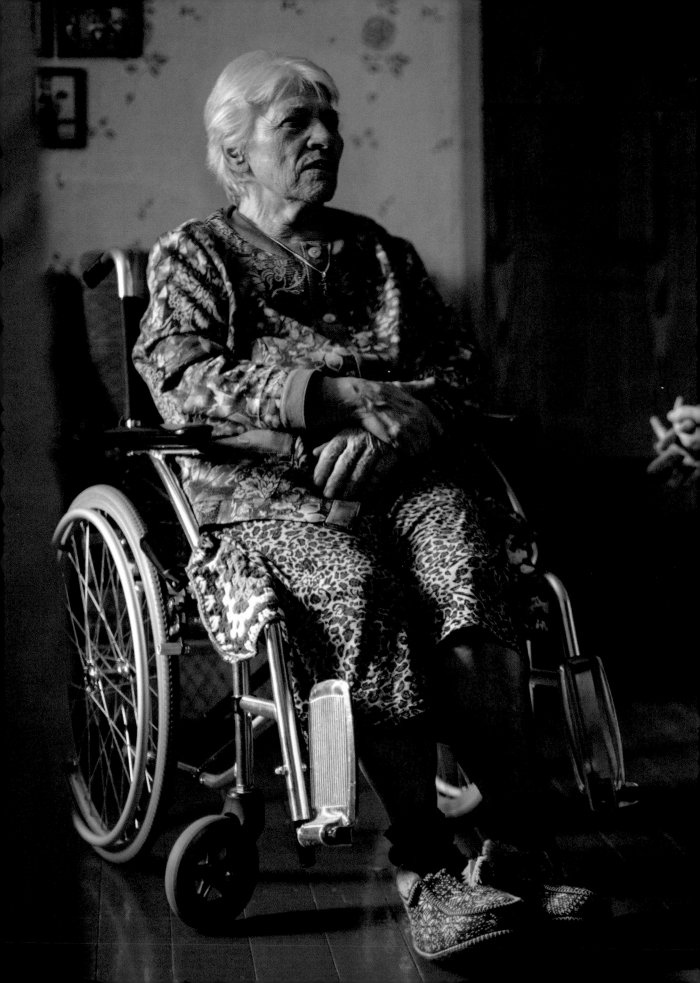

Alla Lutskevich and
her daughter visiting
a parishioner

Ninety-five-year-old Varvara, the oldest parishioner of the Church of Saint Michael, at her home

A theological seminary student in the icon-painting workshop

I chose to focus on Voronezh, a city of one million in the heart of south Russia, where the heritage of Russian Orthodox traditions is treasured and passed from one generation to the next.

I found that women are prominent as leaders and activists in Voronezh's many Orthodox organizations and communities. Since 2003, the wives of Orthodox priests here have helped shape the life of the Voronezh diocese through a women's council, which is the only one of its kind in Russia today. I ask Tatiana Volodko, a *presbytera* or priest's wife and a member of the council *(see next spread)*, why that is. "In other regions, they are reluctant for some reason," she tells me. "Women are too passive."

Surely passivity stems from a misunderstanding of Orthodox humility. True humility should come from within as the crown of the Christian life, not be forced upon women by restrictive traditions that keep them from participating in the life of the church.

In Voronezh, at least, Orthodox women are not holding back. The women I photographed are remarkable for their inner energy and their drive to serve. As I hope my photography conveys, Voronezh's women embody both traditional Orthodox femininity and the plucky spirit of a modern woman. ➤

After the Sunday service, in the church courtyard

Tatiana Volodko, chairwoman of the women's council

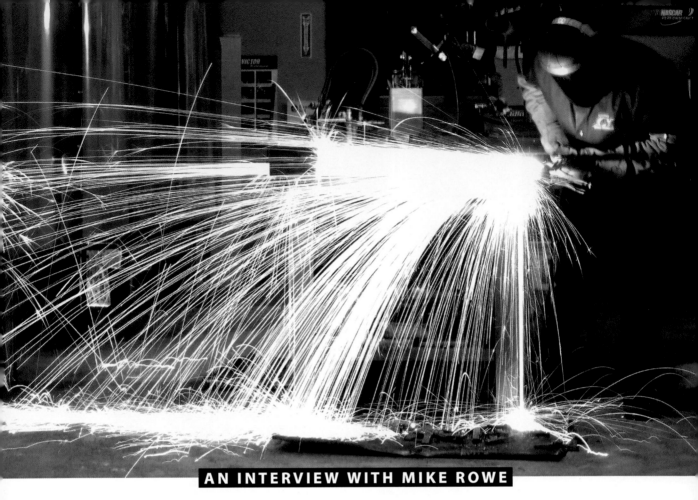

AN INTERVIEW WITH MIKE ROWE

Dirty Work

Mike Rowe hosted the popular Discovery Channel show *Dirty Jobs* and the CNN series *Somebody's Gotta Do It*, apprenticing himself to people who do the hands-on work that keeps civilization running. He talks to *Plough*'s Susannah Black about practical work, why college is overvalued, and how he found redemption in a San Francisco sewer.

Plough: **What's lost if a young person doesn't learn a trade?**

Mike Rowe: Mastering a trade gives you a sense of competency, confidence, and completion. Something positive happens when you get good at doing work that has a beginning and an end. I always knew how I was doing on *Dirty Jobs*, because all I had to do was look to see my progress. People who never go into a trade don't experience the benefit of constant feedback – of always knowing how you're doing.

Mike Rowe is a television host and an activist who promotes blue-collar trades. mikeroweworks.org

Photograph by Mike Rogers

What happened to make your approach seem so radical? Why is this not common sense?

All our choices these days feel binary. If I advocate for one thing, people assume it's because I'm against another. So when I say more people should learn a trade, it often comes back as "Mike is anti-college." That's not true, of course. I'm opposed to unnecessary debt, and I think the cost of a four-year degree is out of control. But arguing in favor of the trades only feels "radical" because it conflicts with the long-held belief that a four-year degree is the best path for the most people.

How did that belief take root?

It's like the frog in the boiling water. It didn't happen overnight. We decided in the sixties that college needed a PR campaign – and it got a really good one. It was the Cold War, we were trying to compete with the USSR, automation was ramping up. We looked around and said, "We need more engineers. We need more big brains doing deep dives into the things you learn in college." And so we went into high schools with a truly silly message: "If you don't go to college, you'll be irrelevant, you'll miss out." We began to promote one form of education at the expense of another. We turned half of our workforce into a cautionary tale. We made trade school into a vocational consolation prize. Throw in a few decades of stereotypical portrayals on TV, and you wind up with a boatload of myths and misperceptions that surround a career in the trades.

A lot of parents seem set on the idea of their kids going to college. Can you talk more about that pressure?

The belief that a college degree is the best path for the most people is deeply held, and it's reinforced every day in countless ways. Today, if a "good parent" sends their kid to a "good school," and the kid winds up indebted or unhappy, the parent – subconsciously – can say, "Well, we did all we could." But did they? Is it really wise to assume that borrowing (or lending) a hundred grand to pursue a liberal arts degree is really the best path for the most people? Nearly half of those who enroll in a four-year school don't finish. They enter the workforce with no degree, and no useful skill. Their debt, however, stays with them.

Mike Rowe

Parents are subjected to the same kind of peer pressure as kids. They don't want to screw their kids up. Their friends are watching. And so, every year, thousands of well-intentioned, otherwise rational parents allow their kids to assume a level of debt they simply can't afford. Maybe that's why the cost of college has risen faster than the cost of energy, food, real estate, and healthcare? Maybe that's why we've got $1.5 trillion in student loans? We're lending money we don't have to kids who aren't going to be able to pay it back to educate them for jobs that don't exist. Meanwhile, we have 7.3 million open jobs, many of which require training – not a degree. Probably time to push back against the pressure.

What kind of exposure did you have to the trades growing up?

Most everyone in my family except my parents, who were schoolteachers, were farmers, fishermen, or tradespeople. My grandfather, who lived next door, was a master electrician – one of those guys who could build a house without a blueprint. He was a genius in his own way, and I was determined to follow in his footsteps.

What happened?

Unfortunately, the handy gene is recessive, and apparently, I didn't get it. It took me a long time to get the message that I was not going to make a living in the trades, but it was my grandfather who gave me a different way to think about things. He said, "Look, Mike, you can be a tradesman, just get a different toolbox." I was seventeen when I started looking at music and acting. While I didn't initially love them, I learned that I was good at them. At least, better than I was at making things. It was a valuable lesson: just because you love something doesn't mean you're going to be good at it, and just because you don't like something initially doesn't mean you shouldn't pursue it.

What did that pursuit look like? What was your first job?

I crashed an audition for the Baltimore Opera and got my union card. That allowed me to audition for roles in television, including a very weird but very instructive job as a host on The QVC Shopping Channel. That experience changed everything. Three years later, I'd accumulated enough skills to book all sorts of work. I became a chronic freelancer, and loved it. I worked for every network, hosted all kinds

Oh, to Weld!

The Satisfactions of Teaching a Trade

MARIO MEIER

As a boy, I admired my Uncle Danni's ability to weld. Something about permanently bonding two pieces of metal together intrigued me: the crackle and blue intensity of the electric arc that he forbade me to look at. It was the late 1970s during what was then called "the fuel crisis," and my uncle was designing and building wood furnaces to heat the homes in the Bruderhof community in upstate New York where he lived. He was a self-taught master, adept at fabricating his own hinges and camlock latches. Watching him, I knew I wanted to weld.

In my high school sophomore year, I signed up for a vocational welding course. My instructor had years of experience in the Steel City industries, along with chilling tales of the dangers of metal-working. We learned all the types of welding and we practiced in all positions. A welder has to conquer gravity to make liquefied steel stay exactly where he wants it – there lies the challenge. When I mastered a specific joint

and earned my teacher's approval of technique and form, I felt proud. A weld is your very own signature. When Keats wrote that "a thing of beauty is a joy forever," he wasn't thinking of a perfect weld, but he could have been.

The next summer my uncle invited me to New York and together we fabricated and welded a large wood boiler. I had become a welder and he trusted me. In his gentle way he was teaching me so much more: about work ethic, manhood, and life. Now I was not just welding plates for practice. Every joint I welded on a water jacket or heat-exchanger pipe had to survive pressure testing. Uncle Danni was testing my mettle and I loved the challenge.

After high school, I took a year of machining technology at a community college north of Pittsburgh. Eventually, I became a Bruderhof member and started working in the community's Rifton Equipment business, which manufactures therapeutic equipment for

Mario Meier is a teacher at the Mount Academy in Esopus, New York, a private high school run by the Bruderhof communities.

of different shows, and narrated hundreds of nature documentaries. If there was a wildebeest being eaten by a crocodile as it tried to cross the Serengeti, I was probably telling you about it.

But along the way, I became slowly disconnected from the things that I grew up with – where my food came from, where my energy came from, work, history; all of the things that I valued as a kid, I began to take for granted.

And then, when I was working at CBS in 2001, my mom called me. "Your grandfather's ninety," she said. "He's not going to be around forever. It would sure be great if he could turn on the television and see you doing something that looks like work." She had a point.

I was hosting a show at the time called *Evening Magazine*. I went to my boss and said, "Look, why does this show always have to be hosted from a winery or a theater opening? Why

people with disabilities. I became a welding instructor in the company. Even after I moved on to other jobs, married, and raised a family of four, I kept using my welding skills to create and fabricate and as a hobby.

Two years ago I came full circle: I'm teaching the new vocational welding program at the Bruderhof's high school, the Mount Academy, in Esopus, New York. A hundred-year-old red brick garage was renovated into a beautiful welding facility.

Now it's my chance to pass on my trade. Every student that enters the course comes with mixed abilities but eager to master this skill I had learned long ago. The most beautiful precision welds are those made by creating an arc with a tungsten electrode and then precisely dabbing a filler rod to create your weld. These TIG welds, mostly made on aluminum or stainless steel, are the kind of precise and uniformly rippled welds you'll find on a well-made

mountain bike. They have a distinctive sheen. When students get feed and speed just right, they can hardly wait to lift their helmets to see their art.

This past semester five of our Welding 2 students competed at the New York State Skills USA Competition. One student did a stunning sculpture of a mythological creature, art being another creative use for welding skills. One student placed high in the individual competition and our three-student team took the Bronze by welding a hexagonal fire pit.

Before they graduate, each student creates a welded name plate which is placed high on our shop's Wall of Fame. They have worked hard to acquire a skill that they will never lose. They take with them, too, the lessons I learned from my Uncle Danni, who died last year: self-discipline, pride in hard work, the dignity of a skilled trade, and a keen appreciation for a beautiful bead.

Photograph by Simon Caspersen/Unsplash

obviously, and called for my immediate dismissal. But others – lots of others – wrote in with invitations. It was always the same thing: "You gotta meet my dad, my brother, my uncle, my cousin, my sister. Wait till you see what *they* do." We were showing work, real work that real people really do, and there was clearly an appetite for more.

Anyway, after ten years of acting like a host, I began to act like an apprentice. I sold that show to the Discovery Channel as *Dirty Jobs*, and that's how I got reconnected to work. But it started with a phone call from mother.

Tell us about why you started your foundation.

By 2008, *Dirty Jobs* was the number one show on Discovery. I think it was the number one show on cable. Then the economy went south. Reporters started asking me to weigh in on all kinds of topics relating to work. They assumed I might have an opinion, and it turns out, I did.

The headlines all talked about unemployment. But everywhere I went, I saw Help Wanted signs. So I thought there might be another story going on in the country, a story about opportunities that go unloved because there aren't enough skilled workers to do them. Why is no one talking about that?

I began to write about things that Dirty Jobbers knew that the rest of us don't; I started talking about the frustrations of employers

can't I go to a construction site or a sewer?"

He said, "Do whatever you want, Mike. Nobody's watching the show anyway."

So I hosted an episode of *Evening Magazine* from a sewer. My guide was a sewer inspector, and together with my cameraman, we crawled through miles of unspeakable filth, and I learned all sorts of things about sewers along the way. It was weird and funny and fascinating. I was also covered in roaches and attacked by a rat. Anyway, that episode aired one night during the dinner hour, and all hell broke loose. Some people were disgusted,

Plough Quarterly ◆ *Autumn 2019*

who were unable to attract skilled workers for good jobs that no one wanted.

So my foundation, mikeroweWorks, began as a PR campaign for opportunities in the skilled trades, and evolved into a scholarship fund. We've given away maybe five or six million dollars in "work-ethic scholarships" to people who want to learn a skill or master a trade. I look for qualified candidates who demonstrate the kind of work ethic we all want to encourage, and do what I can to help them.

What are the things that Dirty Jobbers know that the rest of us don't?

They know that if they all call in sick for a week, civilization goes off the rails. That's something that a lot of people lose sight of: civilization is fragile. And the knowledge that they are essential creates a spirit, something unmistakable. Shakespeare said it: "We few, we happy few, we band of brothers." I found that mentality among construction workers and garbage collectors and on factory floors. They know that the wheels would come off if they sat down on the job.

The thing with the Dirty Jobbers that surprised people was what a good time they were having. They were thriving. As a group, they don't say "Follow your passion." By and large, the people we featured on the show understood that passion is too important to "follow." They brought their passion with them.

Today, on the other hand, we tell our kids that the secret to job satisfaction is to first identify that which makes them happy, and then do whatever it takes to get there. We encourage them to borrow whatever it takes to get their "dream job," as though the job will be the thing that determines their happiness. It's the same thing we tell people about finding their soul mate. The idea that there's only one person out there for you, and if you can just find that one person, then you'll be happy. That rarely works in romance, and it rarely works in the workforce.

With *Dirty Jobs*, we introduced the audience to people who make six figures a year cleaning out septic tanks. People who are passionate about what they do, even though they wind up covered in other people's crap. When I ask those people, "What's the secret to job satisfaction," the answer is never, "I followed my passion into a septic tank." The answer is always, "Well, I looked around and said, 'What job needs doing? Oh, here's an opening.' Then I figured out how to be good at it, and finally, how to enjoy it." That's the difference between following your passion versus bringing your passion with you.

Most people who are passionate about what they do whom I've met didn't follow their dream. They followed opportunity, mastered a useful skill, and then grew to love their job – usually after they got good at it. It's that mix: skill, work ethic, knowing who you are, and knowing that what you're doing is actually moving the needle. All of those qualities make happy people. On *Dirty Jobs*, I met a lot of happy people.

Isn't the approach that you advocate more common in Europe and elsewhere than in America?

It is. In Germany, for example, and in Switzerland and South Korea, there's a heightened sense in the culture that vocational jobs are truly aspirational. That's the key difference – a fundamentally different definition of what a "good job" means, along with a greater enthusiasm for apprenticeship programs and vocational schools. That's not to say we don't have some terrific vocational schools – Williamson College, The New York Harbor School, Dubiski Career High School

Photograph by Christopher Burns/Unsplash

(just outside of Dallas), and plenty of others; trade schools that will teach you welding or electrical wiring. The problem is PR. Most parents don't realize those schools even exist.

You talk a lot about welding.

That's because society is held together with welds; they are the connective tissue. No welds, everything falls apart. About four years ago, a woman applied for a work-ethic scholarship in welding. We got her trained, she found a job, and six months later, she sent me a pipe in the mail. It was actually two pieces of pipe, perfectly welded together. It occurred to me that when somebody sends you a pipe in the mail with a perfect weld on it and a nice thank-you note, you may be doing something right.

Is it fair to say that your work is about the desire to reconnect to the physical world?

You can't reconnect until or unless you first realize you've become disconnected. That's what happened to me. Over time, I became increasingly disconnected from a lot of things that interested me as a young kid in the Boy Scouts. The first few episodes of *Dirty Jobs* brought that to my attention.

If the show has a larger purpose, it's to remind people that blue-collar and white-collar work are not opposites – they're two sides of the same coin. Likewise, the skills gap is not a mystery – it's a reflection of what we value, and what we don't.

I got a bunch of calls in 2016 when Marco Rubio said, during the presidential debate, that we need more welders and fewer philosophers. People were like, "Oh man, he's singing your song!" And I said, actually he's not. It's not one or the other. What we need is more welders who can discuss Kant and Descartes, and we need more philosophers who can run an even bead and repair a leaky faucet. ⤳

Image from Wikimedia Commons (public domain)

EBERHARD ARNOLD

LOVE IS WORK: practical, strenuous work of muscle and mind, heart and soul. The kingdom of love, therefore, must be a kingdom of work. Work, truly unselfish work, animated by the spirit of brotherliness, will be the mark of the future, the character of the mankind to be. Work as spirit, work as living reality, such as we all have lost; work as dedication in enthusiastic love of togetherness – that is the fundamental character of the future. Joy in togetherness will show as joy in work.

How infinitely remote present-day mankind is from work like this! And since today we have only a faint conception of the possibility of this common life, we will be troubled again and again by pessimism.

But we do know that it is not some fantastic, unattainable future; on the contrary, it is the quiet reality of a church already emerging today. . . . Just this is the mystery of the emerging church, germinating and blossoming among us in secret – that we can live and work already now, here and everywhere, in the community of the Spirit.

DOROTHY SAYERS

THE MODERN TENDENCY seems to be to identify work with gainful employment; and this is, I maintain, the essential heresy. . . . The fallacy being that work is not the expression of man's creative energy in the service of Society, but only something he does in order to obtain money and leisure.

We urgently need a Christian doctrine of work, which shall provide, not only for proper conditions of employment, but also that the work shall be such as a man may do with his whole heart, and that he shall do it for the very work's sake. But we cannot expect a sacramental attitude to work, while many people are forced, by our evil standard of values, to do work which is a spiritual degradation – a long series of financial trickeries, for example, or the manufacture of vulgar and useless trivialities.

GERARD MANLEY HOPKINS

IT IS NOT ONLY PRAYER that gives God glory but work. Smiting on an anvil, sawing a beam, whitewashing a wall, driving horses, sweeping, scouring, everything gives God some glory if being in his grace you do it as your duty. To go to communion worthily gives God great glory, but to take food in thankfulness and temperance gives him glory too. To lift up the hands in prayer gives God glory, but a man with a dungfork in his hand, a woman with a slop pail, gives him glory too. He is so great that all things give him glory if you mean they should. So then, my brethren, live. ➤

Georges Seurat, *Farm Women at Work*, detail, oil on canvas, 1882

Sources: *Eberhard Arnold (Modern Spiritual Masters)*, (Orbis, 2005), 121 122; Dorothy Sayers, *Creed or Chaos* (Methuen, 1947), 68; *Poems and Prose of Gerard Manley Hopkins*, ed. W. H. Gardner (Penguin, 1953), 146.

Julian Peters is an illustrator and comic book artist living in Montreal, Canada, who focuses on adapting classical poems into graphic art. This visual interpretation is taken from Peters's upcoming collection Poems to See By *(Plough, 2020).*

THE BUFFALOES ARE GONE.

AND THOSE WHO SAW THE BUFFALOES ARE GONE.

THOSE WHO SAW THE BUFFALOES BY THOUSANDS AND HOW THEY PAWED THE PRAIRIE SOD

INTO DUST WITH THEIR HOOFS, THEIR GREAT HEADS DOWN PAWING ON IN A GREAT PAGEANT OF DUSK,

THOSE WHO SAW THE BUFFALOES ARE GONE.

AND THE BUFFALOES ARE GONE.

I HAVE MEMORIES from my first deployment to Iraq that are unclassifiable: memories that destabilize my certainty about the world. One of the strongest of these is of being on tower guard – which is exactly what it sounds like – and watching American mercenaries roll out of the gate to go on a mission.

Of course they didn't call themselves mercenaries, but instead used the more neutral term *contractor*. Most of them had formerly served in the US armed forces. Many had been exactly where we were, looking down from an observation point in a tower, guarding a base, bored from scanning the horizon and having long since run out of things to talk about with the person next to them.

We shared so much in common: Americans in a war zone, sleeping only yards from one another. And yet I had a real animosity for them. Every similarity we shared felt negated by the fact that we were *real* soldiers, and they were opportunists – paid more than we were for doing the same job. We risked our lives for honor, out of a sense of duty. They fought for money.

The hiring of mercenaries has an ancient, if not entirely venerable, history. Mercenaries were employed by the Roman Empire, of course. The European Middle Ages were rife with troops who were often little more than hired thugs – also known as "contractors," *condottieri*. When their employers couldn't pay them outright, mercenaries were promised plunder, which typically came from the innocents unfortunate enough to live in the army's path. It wasn't until the seventeenth century that state-run armies began gradually to replace mercenaries. Sean McFate, a former paratrooper and private defense contractor who now teaches foreign policy at Georgetown University, writes in *The Modern Mercenary*:

> By 1650, it was clear that on-demand military services were no longer economical to rulers, given the destruction that mercenaries wrought upon the countryside and the threat they posed to their employers. What was needed was a public army of systematically trained and disciplined professionals, maintained in peace and war, winter and summer, with a regular means of obtaining supplies and replacements. Critically, this military force would be paid by, and loyal to, the state.

This notion carried on into the Enlightenment, as the modern nation-state became inextricably bound up with its military. Immanuel Kant's 1795 pamphlet *Perpetual Peace: A Philosophical Sketch*, often taken to be the blueprint for modern liberal thought, theorizes the eventual eradication of war by the creation of citizen armies. If the decision is left to a coterie of nobles, Kant reasons, then warring is done "without any significant reason, as a kind of amusement." And mercenaries, according to Kant, are "mere machines" with a vested economic interest in ongoing hostilities. Citizens, on the other hand, would surely only choose to go to war themselves in cases of absolute necessity. As Daniel Moran explains in his book *The People in Arms*, "Because [republics] were founded upon universal values and the consent of the governed, they could respond directly to mankind's natural preference for peace and prosperity over war and penury." Kant's thinking was that lasting peace would require citizens to have their own skin in the game, so to speak, in order to avoid unnecessary aggression.

Scott Beauchamp is a writer and veteran whose work has appeared in the Paris Review, *the* Atlantic, *and* New York Magazine. *His book* Did You Kill Anyone? *is forthcoming from Zero Books. He lives in Maine.*

Of course, the history of the twentieth century calls into question Kant's rosy theorizing. With democracies maintaining powerful militaries, wars only got larger and deadlier, with more bodies thrown into the meat grinder. But this sort of political reasoning persists. After all, in a democracy, whether or not they have much skin in the game personally, citizens themselves – via their elected representatives – do influence when we go to war.

Another vestige of the Kantian ideal is the image of the noble citizen soldier. A soldier fighting for a nation is on higher moral ground than a mere "sellsword." The ideal of private honor, which in the Renaissance led to the private mini-wars called duels, transformed into the ideal of public honor. To fight for one's nation as a soldier was honorable. To fight only for money became the ultimate mark of dishonor.

In reality, despite our Enlightenment ideals, most of America's military excursions haven't passed the democratic test. Though "private interest" now refers to the profit of corporations instead of local lords, the line between private interest and public resources (soldiers and tax dollars) remains blurred. The distinction became functionally irrelevant during World War II, thanks to the top-secret Manhattan Project that created the atomic bomb. As Garry Wills writes in his book *Bomb Power*:

> For the first time in our history, the president was given sole and unconstrained authority over all possible uses of the Bomb. All the preparations, protections, and auxiliary requirements for the Bomb's use, including secrecy about the whole matter and a worldwide deployment of various means of delivery,

launching by land, sea, air, or space – a vast network for the study, development, creation, storage, guarding, and updating of nuclear arsenals, along with an immense intelligence apparatus to ascertain conditions for the weapons' maintenance and employment – all these were concentrated in the executive branch, immune from interference by the legislative or judicial branches. Every executive encroachment or abuse was liable to justification from this one supreme power.

Indeed, the creation of the bomb itself, Wills explains, necessitated a parallel, secret government that could draw on vast public and private resources well out of the watchful public eye. When the war eventually ended, this parallel infrastructure of national defense cannibalized our democratically controlled military, replacing it with the military-industrial complex that Eisenhower warned about in his farewell address.

The moral drawbacks of maintaining a public-private hybrid defense system that is untethered from public control bear a direct relation to the material drawbacks. Mandy Smithberger from the Project on Government Oversight explained this to me:

> Decisions about where we go to war, what services and weapons we buy, and where we otherwise deploy forces should be based on our national security interests, and ideally the most cost-effective way to advance those goals. When the military and the Pentagon become too close to defense contractors it becomes too easy to conflate what benefits those companies – big budgets, endless war, and reduced oversight – with what is truly in the public interest.

To fight for one's nation as a soldier was honorable. To fight only for money became the ultimate mark of dishonor.

The term "public interest" has been largely emptied of its significance by proponents of excessive defense budgets. In 2015, US military spending accounted for nearly six hundred billion dollars, or 54 percent of all federal discretionary spending. Defenders of big military budgets argue that this contributes to the economic well-being of the country, pointing to its contribution to the gross domestic product (GDP). But a 2017 study of one hundred and seventy countries over forty-five years, published in the journal *Defense and Peace Economics*, undermines this claim. It finds that, across the board, increased military spending negatively impacted a country's economic growth. And even if high defense spending bolstered GDP, that's not enough to prove that it is in the public interest. GDP is a notoriously poor tool for assessing the public interest: after all, it counts natural disasters as

economic positives while ignoring vital aspects of human flourishing, such as leisure time and equitable distribution of resources. Funneling vast public resources into a military-industrial complex largely sheltered from democratic oversight might cause GDP to rise, but so might an earthquake or a hurricane. This is the wrong way to measure the common good.

Nevertheless, big budgets and endless war have been the predominant experience of the American military since World War II. And as public involvement in war making and intelligence gathering has receded, the trend of privatizing our defenses continues unabated, despite much-publicized scandals. In 2009, according to McFate, the ratio of contractors to US troops in war zones was one to one; it is now roughly three to one. Tim Shorrock, author of *Spies for Hire,* writes in the *New York Times*: "These companies are deeply engaged in

Blackwater USA contractors engage in a firefight with Iraqi insurgents, April 4, 2004.

Corporal Daniel Hopping, assaultman, during a mission in Afghanistan, April 28, 2014

countries dependent on mining and extractive industries. . . . Their deployment, coupled with extensive use of intelligence and surveillance contractors, makes it possible for the United States to pursue wars on the sly. Who besides their families keeps track of contractor deaths – estimated at over six thousand in Iraq and Afghanistan – on the battlefield?"

Shorrock's point about contractors in countries dependent on extractive industries reveals another aspect of this trend: mercenary companies employed by the US government for counterterrorism work are often simultaneously hired by the local government, a local warlord, or another private corporation to guard mines and industrial plants. These industries tend to have the worst human rights records, and persistent corruption.

Erik Prince, founder of the notorious private military company Blackwater, seems persistently drawn to these business opportunities: this year, he's been aiming to go into cobalt mining in central Africa. In a region with no effective national governance, such an enterprise must somehow combine business, private government, and private military: a sort of corporate state, in fact, which Prince claims would benefit those under its hand.

There is an effort afoot to create a firmer border between private firms and our public defense organizations. Yet the difficulty in establishing where this line lies indicates that there is something even bigger and more insidious at play. When the Pentagon is untethered from common notions of when combat is absolutely required and when it is not, its animating logic too often comes to mirror the logic of capitalism itself.

"Most taxpayers seriously think 'defense' of the country is the basic task of the military,"

John Dolan, who writes military analysis under the pen name Gary Brecher and runs the *War Nerd* podcast, explained to me recently. "But that hasn't been the plan for a long time. The US military is de facto an instrument of interventionist foreign policy. Its job is to enforce policy, usually very dumb policy, around the world, particularly in the Middle East and North Africa and to a lesser extent in sub-Saharan Africa."

"The big problem for a profit-based military," Dolan added, "which is what 'private' means here, is that it might someday have to fight a real war. And when it does, it will find that profit isn't much use. Why are we buying the useless, obscenely expensive F-35, when much cheaper planes like the A-10 and F-16 do its jobs much better? Because there's more money in a bad plane, which will generate far more profit in decades of urgent, price-gouged repairs and refits than even its $1.4 *trillion* initial price tag." (Dolan was referring to the official projected cost of the F-35 program over its fifty-five-year lifetime.)

To put it plainly, we have a military whose primary motive is to metastasize, not serve the people. It is here that its resemblance to capitalism is most plain: both are unyoked from any guiding moral principles and constantly seek to move beyond physical or ideological limits.

A striking illustration of this is the new technologies the US military is spearheading. For instance, the Department of Defense is creating prototypes of direct brain-to-machine interfacing, and overseeing trials "using mind-controlled drones for use by the military." It's also pioneering new ways for artificial intelligence to predict which people holding security clearances might breach security protocols – a

military parallel to the "predictive policing" now employed in several American cities. As Patrick Tucker writes at *Defense One*, "the goal is not just to detect employees who have betrayed their trust, but to predict which ones might – allowing problems to be resolved with calm conversation rather than punishment." He goes on to call this the future of human resources.

Capitalism and the military *want*, for lack of a better term, the same things. Both want intrusive intelligence and data gathering for purposes of control. Both wish to replace thinking with mechanical calculation, meaning and purpose with accumulation. And perhaps most importantly, both want to "reduce humans themselves to functional elements in a system," as the philosopher Byung-Chul Han writes. "Capitalist production is aimless," Han states in his book *The Agony of Eros*. "It no longer has any concern for the *good* life." A military unmoored from any hard definition of necessity, unaccountable to the people it serves, takes on these same nihilistic characteristics.

Were the mercenaries just a more honest version of what I was?

I surely wasn't thinking about all these things when I was standing in my guard tower back in Iraq, watching the mercenaries roll out of the gate. I was just awash in strong emotion. I felt disdain at what I perceived was, for lack of a better word, such a dishonorable profession.

But in retrospect, that revulsion was tempered by a barely perceptible notion that perhaps I wasn't all that different from them. That maybe they were just a more honest version of what I was, and that the oath I took and the creeds I followed only camouflaged the true nature of our endeavor. Maybe I hated them for making it so obvious. ⌦

To-Do List

For in relation to the absolute there is only one tense: the present.
—Søren Kierkegaard

On my to-do list, like pulling the clematis
from the yard, waist-high tangles
that would've been easier to yank
years ago. For now, it creeps
echoing the mildew inside
on ceiling and walls. One gets accustomed
to the smell, to stumbling when playing
with the dog. One accommodates,
as when the cheap handyman laid
a crooked floor, learning
not to trip in the dark. As long as
a single sink works, one can wash
one's hands of the business.

DEVON BALWIT

Loneliness at College

PETER BILES

In a crowded café in northern Illinois, I sipped coffee and gazed out of windows blurred with drizzle. I was kept afloat by caffeine, but desperate for real rest. It had been gray and raining for days, a mild but sordid winter. The allure of snowdrifts and blustery college days had once been enchanting, but this drab, chilly world just piled on to an even deeper disappointment.

When I arrived at Wheaton College, a Christian liberal arts school an hour outside Chicago, I wasn't exactly sure what to expect, but I knew what I *needed*: a good community. And this college seemed to guarantee I'd get it. Most universities portray their campuses as communal havens, but Wheaton attracted me with its explicitly Christian model. I imagined that by Christmas of my freshman year I would

Harley Manifold, *Summer Sun*, oil on Belgian linen

Peter Biles is a senior at Wheaton College in Illinois. In summer 2019 he was an editorial intern for Plough.

be deeply embedded in a community of like-minded peers. Yet months passed and there I was, an isolate with society teeming all around me. It seemed like we were all living in a world of personas, prepped and pretty and "spiritual," smiling and interacting, but never connecting. I was a performer in an endless play, and our masks were never discarded to show our true faces. My acknowledged need for community became confused with a quest for

---

In my loneliness, I was hardly alone.

---

validation from other people, from God, and even from myself. The desire for intimacy was shortchanged by a toxic demand for approval without the vulnerability of real relationships. My world resembled the one social media offers: an ideal façade hiding the underlying sin.

Over time my expectations of communal life at Wheaton began to fade. Phrases like "flourishing community" and "vibrant, intentional living" turned into wispy fairy tales. I had wanted it to revolve around my needs, and it failed. That dreary day I was forced to ask myself an honest question: "Does anyone here know who I really am? And does anyone here feel known by *me*?"

In my loneliness, I was hardly alone. In January 2019 NBC reported that the average

American has only one close friend, and today's teenagers and college students are the loneliest of any age group. Countless college students drift through the whole four years without disclosing themselves to another person, only to find themselves thrust out into a larger world also lacking community. The typical college environment, billed as a very social space, is not actually well suited to encourage relational flourishing. Contemporary universities, particularly ones with high academic standards, tend to revolve around competition, image, and merit by default, functioning as more of a social ladder than a social community.

Of course no university wishes its students to be lonely. Some colleges do make special efforts to grapple with student isolation. Cornell University has the Chesterton House, an intentional community of students and recent grads seeking to share life and ideas together. Wheaton is home to the Shalom House, a multiethnic group intended to traverse cultural differences and live together in Christ. Well-funded student-life programming at any number of schools at least attempts to realize the neatly packaged, joy-filled communal experience they advertise. Rather than blaming universities for failing to deliver on these ideal visions, we would do better to recognize that the problem of loneliness and disconnection strikes a deeper nerve.

In the spring of my sophomore year, during a personal low of isolation, the Wheaton philosophy department offered a special course on existentialism. Along with twenty other students, I read some of the best literature in the world reckoning with loneliness, love, God, shame, and death. For us the class was not just an academic exercise, but a personal opportunity to grapple with the fundamental pains and potential of existence.

Harley Manifold, *Summer Shade*, oil on board

David Foster Wallace's *Infinite Jest* dominated the course. This hefty, complex novel revolves around a simple problem: inner "aloneness" and the addictions people use to cope with it. The book hit me like a hammer. In describing a main character's spiritual condition, Wallace writes, "Forget so-called peer-pressure. It's more like peer-hunger. No? We enter a spiritual puberty where we snap to the fact that the great transcendent horror is *loneliness*, excluded encagement in the self. Once we've hit this age, we will now give or take anything, wear any mask, to fit, be part-of, not be Alone, we young."

Wallace describes how drug addicts seek to recover from their isolation and addiction through twelve-step groups. These programs demand brutal honesty, recognizing one's "rock bottom" condition, submitting to God (or a "higher power") and walking through the struggle to healing arm in arm.

Most of us agreed that this is not the traditional approach to community, either in secular or evangelical cultures. College campuses and churches are not generally portrayed as spaces for addicts in recovery. Nonetheless, the class had me wondering what addictions in our own lives might be blocking the deep connections we longed for. Social media is one common culprit. "Sites like Facebook promise to connect us to friends," writes Jean Twenge in a 2017 *Atlantic* article, but the data show instead "a lonely, dislocated generation." Teens experience heightened feelings of isolation while spending

Harley Manifold, *Echoes,* oil on Belgian linen

inordinate amounts of time online, feeling left out and disconnected despite being so digitally "in touch" with their peers.

Another hazard of the internet is unlimited access to pornography. Wallace himself, writing in the late nineties, foresaw the explosion of porn online. While it's often not talked about openly, particularly at a religious campus such as Wheaton, porn addiction is poisoning relationships across the board. In my own life and in the lives of some of the people dearest to me, I've seen the pain and distortion it can cause. Both men and women are increasingly viewing it – not only in replacement for romantic vulnerability, but to somehow make up for a general lack of human intimacy. My classmates and I viewed it because we were already feeling disconnected in some

inarticulable way. In this way, addictions and coping mechanisms, engaged in to evoke the illusion of security and intimacy, increase the isolation.

Though the course on existentialism was revelatory, it didn't bring us all the way into community with each other. But it did plot a milestone in my understanding of loneliness. And the questions of addiction, isolation, and God we wrestled with unexpectedly led me back to the story of Adam and Eve. While familiar with the story, I had never plumbed its complexities and psychological depth until I encountered a small painting in the hallway of a campus building. The painting was *Adam and Eve Are Banished from Paradise* by Marc Chagall, a Jewish artist from the twentieth century who specialized in flowing, colorful pictures. It depicts the distraught figures of the first couple, bowed under the sword of an angel as they make their way east of Eden and into the world, having lost the interactive presence of God and their open trust in each other. In its essence, the painting communicates a deep loneliness and rejection, capturing the scope of the story with just a few brush strokes. These people, I thought, are us.

Like Adam and Eve and the addicts in *Infinite Jest*, we each have something shameful to hide, and we're afraid to show it for fear of rejection. The communities formed among such people can look cheery on the outside, but remain fragile and insecure, riddled with gossip and judgments. When there's pressure to perform such as there is on college campuses, students will very likely opt for these unhealthy outlets over deeper human connections, and the few connections they do manage will be tainted with pretense. As John Coe and Todd Hall write in their 2010 book *Psychology of the Spirit*, "A false self that is hiding and covering, pretending to be shiny, cannot really love or be loved, for it is not the actual self that is present but a phantom of a self." Jesus himself spoke of the impulse to hide: "For everyone who does evil hates the light, and does not come to the light for fear that his deeds will be exposed" (John 3:20). When my question changed from "Why is there loneliness on campuses?" to "Why are we so bent on hiding from each other?" a world of insight opened to me.

My isolation at Wheaton taught me that I've always been a "hider." My politeness and courtesy growing up gave me a reputation as a "good guy," but in college the shell I'd worn for so long ended up suffocating any real personality and joy. Eventually, even family, religion, and personal interests couldn't overcome the failures, weaknesses, and wounds of my inner

> There's a limit to how long a person can "dress up" for others and for God. Sooner or later the real mess has to surface.

life. There's a limit to how long a person can "dress up" for others and for God. Sooner or later the real mess has to surface. Yet it is in the light that everything can change. The words of 1 John point the way: "If we walk in the light as he himself is in the light, we have fellowship with one another, and the blood of Jesus his Son cleanses us from all sin" (1 John 1:7).

To give and receive genuine love takes grueling honesty and penitence. What exactly did I have to repent of? While subtle and hard to unmask, my sin was shutting myself off to love I hadn't "earned." It was an inverted self-absorption. I had to learn the humility to receive grace, and in turn be able to give it. It was here, in my brokenness, that I found true communion.

There was a group of juniors who lived together in an apartment near campus. One of them, Noah, simply began inviting me over. These guys weren't part of an intentional program and were notably different in personality and interests, but they acted as a brotherly unit, and hospitably included me. I learned to listen to *their* problems and pains instead of focusing on my own. I started to love other human beings as they are. I experienced Christ through these people. With time and grace, I found myself a new person.

A year later we were all groomsmen in Noah's wedding. The day honored the bond Noah and his wife, Rebecca, had built during their time at Wheaton, extending from the mutual support of our community. As an isolated freshman, wondering what I was doing in life, I had never dreamed of being part of such a sacred moment. I reflected on how far God had taken me.

Our little band of brethren reminded each other of a great truth that needs retelling in our sad and lonely age. Christianity teaches that through Jesus we are absolved of all sin, and so no longer have any need to hide. Those who behold the gospel without hiding behind a wall of shame or self-righteousness are risen to a new life and given the spirit of God to develop a character able to love others as we are first loved. College promised me community, but it was God who delivered it. ⤙

Lightly men talk of saying what they mean. Often when he was teaching me to write in Greek the Fox would say, "Child, to say the very thing you really mean, the whole of it, nothing more or less or other than what you really mean; that's the whole art and joy of words." A glib saying. When the time comes to you at which you will be forced at last to utter the speech which has lain at the center of your soul for years, which you have, all that time, idiot-like, been saying over and over, you'll not talk about joy of words. I saw well why the gods do not speak to us openly, nor let us answer. Till that word can be dug out of us, why should they hear the babble that we think we mean? How can they meet us face to face till we have faces?

—C. S. Lewis, *Till We Have Faces*

An Economy for Anything

NATHAN SCHNEIDER

Can visionary cryptocurrency wonks break the hold of conventional politics and economics?

FIRST HEARD about the digital currency Bitcoin while reporting at an Occupy Wall Street gathering in 2011, and I didn't care. Who needed another kind of money, even an anarchist-sounding kind that needed no government to issue it? The better parts of the Occupy movement were about what people were doing *without* money: serving vast amounts of food, making art, building usable software, and having bottomless conversations.

Then, in early 2014, an old friend took me aside to tell me about this new thing happening. Like Bitcoin it was based on blockchain technology: a secure network under the control of its users, rather than any central authority. But while Bitcoin used a blockchain ledger to track the exchange of cryptocurrency,

a white paper by a nineteen-year-old named Vitalik Buterin set out to do something more.

Ethereum wasn't just about money. Where Bitcoin records mere transactions, Ethereum would record self-executing contracts. The prospect of virtual organizations set my mind racing about how the dreams of radicals and visionaries I'd been following could be made real in code. People would soon start coding in Ethereum things that used to be the purview of governments, like marriage contracts and secure identity systems. Trying new rules for society could be as easy as publishing a website. This could be a new laboratory for democracy, with endless, permissionless experiments in participation supplanting, from below, the tired, old in-person republics.

Nathan Schneider is a journalist and professor of media studies at the University of Colorado Boulder. His most recent book is Everything for Everyone: The Radical Tradition that Is Shaping the Next Economy *(Nation, 2018).*

I finally met Buterin some months later. It was at the Bitcoin Center, a gaudy storefront a few doors down Broad Street from the New York Stock Exchange. He delivered a nearly hour-long monologue on the bit of game theory then keeping him up at night, barely moving except for the ballet of his bony fingers. Afterward we spoke in the street outside. He endured the chit-chat out of kindness, but such interactions were evidently draining and contrary to his nature, so I didn't prolong it.

That was a street I had gotten to know well during the Occupy protests. The memories haunted me: surely this whole blockchain thing could aspire to something better than being another contender vying for usurious riches in the Financial District. What if, instead of storming the kingdom of high finance, we set out to make networks where money matters less?

I WASN'T ALONE in longing for blockchain democracies, but before long the financiers drowned us out. The demographics of Bitcoin gatherings shifted from geeky, techie white guys to white guys with ties still half-tied from their day jobs at banks. In blockchain ledgers they saw the opportunity to bring derivatives and futures markets and automated trading out of their office towers into everyday life.

Before blockchains, I had never bothered with currency trading outside of border crossings. But during the great 2017 cryptocurrency bubble, I found myself obsessively watching the markets wobble, minute to minute, and placing bets as the value of the virtual tokens I'd obtained while reporting swelled from a night in a hotel room to a year's salary. And then it was gone again. Initial coin offerings blew up and burst, taking fools (who were all of us) with them. The thing

these blockchains have most effectively democratized so far is the soul-crushing subjectivity of the day trader.

AMONG THE FIRST pronouncements of Satoshi Nakamoto, the mysterious inventor of Bitcoin, one finds an urge to supplant political and bureaucratic institutions with economics. Nakamoto fretted about the trust wrongly invested in central banks and their political whims. In their place, Nakamoto offered a system with a fixed, predictable money supply. "The promise of crypto was freedom, not more politics," writes one enthusiast in a recent blog post. The path? "100 Percent Pure Economics."

This further elaborates the libertarian "Californian ideology" that has tended to dominate Internet culture, particularly in Silicon Valley. Internet pioneer John Perry Barlow famously declared in his 1996 rebuke to the governments of the world at Davos, "I declare the global social space we are building to be naturally independent of the tyrannies you seek to impose on us." Instead, in place of elected governments we got venture capitalists. The market would be their rising polity.

It might seem like an apotheosis of this view appears in Eric Posner and Glen Weyl's 2018 book *Radical Markets,* a series of proposals for how our most thorny political problems might be solved if ideology gave way to transactions. It is an original, assumption-twisting work of social science fiction. For instance, the authors argue that enabling voters to literally buy votes, according to certain clever mechanisms, allows them to express their preferences more precisely. Rather than leaving migration to a bureaucratic labyrinth, it could become a new market for indentured servitude. All property, the book suggests, should be unownable and perpetually for sale at a self-assessed, taxable valuation. Just when it all starts to sound like a nightmarish apocalypse, Posner and Weyl contend that these more efficient markets will free up wealth and time and opportunity for non-economic sorts of human flourishing. All the transactions would fade into an automated background.

Since Congress is not likely to reorganize property rights anytime soon, the most plausible testing ground for such proposals may be the virtual, programmable territory of blockchains. Weyl, who holds posts at Microsoft and Princeton, has since joined with Vitalik Buterin to declare the promise of "liberation through radical decentralization."

I F PHILOSOPHY WAS the queen of sciences in the ancient world and theology was in the Middle Ages, followed by a regency for physics, then economics wears the crown today. Other forms of inquiry derive value from the degree that they can be useful tributaries – imparting nuance, even correctives, to her models. Economics is the arbiter of good government, the constraint on what social possibilities are thinkable and sayable. According to the popular Freakonomics franchise, her methods are applicable to every aspect of life. Problems once mired in foolish political, social, and ethical concerns can finally be clarified, rationalized, and settled when translated into economic terms.

The insights and fascinations of such economic universalism are plenty, but they seem to depart from an older aspiration of economic thought: to disappear. John Maynard Keynes, for one, longed for a time when economists might "manage to get themselves thought of as humble, competent people, on the level of dentists."

What if economics were to become a mainly solved problem, at work in the background, but not requiring much attention? It could be, for instance, like running water in wealthier parts of the world, like powered flight, or like polio.

Among people actually interested in solving the economic problem, there are two basic ideas for how to get there. One strategy seeks more equitable sharing of the world's goods by political fiat, perhaps thanks to a workers' revolution or benevolent dictatorship. The other calls for ratcheting up economics itself – churning out so much efficiency that the resulting production makes scarcity no longer a pressing concern.

The eclipse of economics is not merely an aspiration for the future. Hannah Arendt's retelling of ancient Athenian life in *The Human Condition* casts economy as merely "a not too important part of ethics and politics." The word *oeconomica* itself means "household management," and that private affair is the guiding metaphor of Aristotle's book that gave the discipline its name.

Classical Athens was a world in which scarcity existed, to be sure. Yet that scarcity was

organized and orchestrated in such a way so as not to be a pressing question, particularly for the owning class that had the right to participate in politics. The women and slaves who felt scarcity most directly did not have such rights. Economics was the silent premise of politics, not its subject; to be trustworthy in politics, rather than forever suspect of corruption, one's economics had to be already in order. Medieval scarcity, in turn, had its teeth dulled by precisely the spaces that banished economic logic – the common pasture, the common forest, the cathedral.

These are not necessarily pasts to which most of us would want to return. The economic achievements of recent centuries has midwifed wonders, including sufficient wealth and opportunity to curb slavery and the subjugation of women, though these evils remain far from abolished. Economics describes and orchestrates the conditions of possibility for our appliances, our skyscrapers, and our app stores like no other field can. As the philosopher André Gorz put it, "Industrial capitalism was only able to take off when economic rationality freed itself from all the other principles of rationality."

Democracy has fallen victim to that economic rationality. Political theorist Wendy Brown, for instance, speaks of the "hollowing out" that befalls our political selves as more and more areas of our life become economized. The end of the Cold War, rather than ushering in a democratic-capitalist triumph, has delivered an ever more frail, reactive, unresponsive kind of politics, where principle has given way to spectacle. Even as the Dow Jones Industrial Average soars, resentment deepens. The metrics don't represent us.

Blockchains could lend to economics even greater freedom, greater autonomy from other considerations, and greater power. Yet what doesn't fit on their cryptographic ledgers doesn't fit into their world. To trade politics for economics means giving up the parts of us that can't be quantified. Economics still might be a problem to be solved, rather than the solution to all problems. Then, a better kind of politics could begin.

I DIDN'T ENCOUNTER Vitalik Buterin again until this past March. Glen Weyl and a team of volunteers organized a conference in Detroit, RadicalxChange, based on the ideas about radical markets he, Buterin, and others had been developing. About four hundred people attended. (I was an invited speaker.) The Ethereum founder was by that point considerably wealthier but essentially the same gentle, brilliant, utterly mind-absorbed person I remembered. We shared a car one morning from the hotel to the venue, and as he thumbed messages into his phone I asked him what was front-of-mind at the moment. "Public goods provision," he said.

His reply was less cryptic than it sounds. Two nights earlier I'd been in another car, packed with Ethereum developers belting out their opinions on the matter. Their goal was to inscribe into future versions of Ethereum a mechanism that could automatically fund development of the core open-source software. In an essentially rational-choice economic system, they had to persuade self-interested stakeholders to contribute collectively to the common good. This was proving difficult. The coder boys complained that the Ethereum Foundation had become impossibly bureaucratic. They had to act like politicians, reinventing old-world partisan habits on Telegram, the ubiquitous messaging app among blockchain enthusiasts.

The cryptocurrency bubble had burst and a "crypto winter" set in. The value of Ethereum's tokens was now one-tenth of what they were worth in January 2018. The time of "Lambos" (frivolous nouveaux riches, piling up Lamborghinis) was over. Frantic rallying cries to "HODL" (hold your tokens and avert a sell-off) had given way to the call to "BUIDL" (build software that might actually be useful). Ethereum's first run as a playground for unregulated magic money had been astonishingly inefficient, at least by a measure of non-scam productivity. The pretense to governance on blockchains was for the most part a widely acknowledged failure, at least so far. But some saw hope in precisely the domain of human activity this technology was intended to render obsolete: politics. According to an essay by a researcher at a blockchain investment fund, Outlier Ventures, "We aren't just building economies, so economics alone won't work. We are building global communities, so I'm afraid, we are going to need politics."

The rediscovery of the political came for Glen Weyl, too. As Zoë Hitzig, a Harvard graduate student, put it in a tweet to him in January, "Mechanism design needs to house – rather than displace – politics." By then, her critique had folded into collaboration with Weyl and Buterin.

RadicalxChange, in the end, was better than an economics conference. It featured spoken-word poetry, film screenings, science-fiction writing exercises, and a Monopoly game night – the rules modified with one of Weyl's mechanism proposals. A toddler practiced walking in the halls. Among the speakers were rapper and filmmaker Boots Riley and veteran Detroit activist Tawana "Honeycomb" Petty. The volunteer organizers drafted a mission statement calling for nonviolently supplanting capitalism with better markets, plus egalitarianism and community. Weyl hadn't seen the statement before it went on the screen in Detroit, but I overheard him say afterward he loved it. In his main-stage speech, Buterin noted some lessons that the blockchain "cypherpunks" had learned over the years. One was that "money is a fundamentally social thing," that making it work is "all very political." The headline at a crypto-news website ran, "Vitalik Buterin Is Embracing a New Role: Political Theorist."

I admit I have a penchant for the farfetched. Blockchains and radical markets and their ilk are still far from infiltrating the prevailing way of things, if they ever will. Yet such fixations have lent me a close-up glimpse of the near future enough times that I keep at it. In following these particular Babel-like attempts to build up a virtual world from scratch, from white papers to billion-dollar valuations to subsequent collapse, I detect traces of ordinary goodness, and old-fashioned politics, still lurking. Even when we depart as far as we can imagine from our humanness as we know it, we find it there again, more unshakably than before. ⬈

The Artist of Memory

STEPHANIE SALDAÑA

An Iraqi Christian painter conserves glimpses of a world that war destroyed.

Sami Lalu Jahola, *Bride of Qaraqosh*

WHEN THE ISLAMIC STATE invaded the ancient Christian city of Qaraqosh in Iraq on August 6, 2014, the nearly fifty thousand inhabitants all fled: mothers and children, priests and nuns, engineers and farmers and musicians. Among them was Sami Lalu Jahola, an elderly artist who had spent his life painting the sacred art hanging in many of the city's churches. Though he and his family escaped, nearly all his art was left behind and systematically destroyed.

By the time I met him, three years later, he was living as a refugee in Jordan, and all that remained of his annihilated paintings were their photographs. Yet as I came to know his collection, taking in the images of Mary and Jesus, the particular saints venerated in his birthplace, and the women of Qaraqosh adorned in their traditional costumes, I began to understand that a photograph of a destroyed painting can become its own work of art: a memory-scape that outlasts the world it depicted, a beauty that survives its own destruction. The faces within these photos become all the more powerful for carrying the burden of what has happened to them. With both his paintings and photographs I have come to think of Sami Lalu as an accidental artist of memory – a recorder of that which has vanished, but also remains. As the poet W. S. Merwin wrote: "What you remember is saved."

Stephanie Saldaña is a writer based in the Middle East and the author of, most recently, A Country Between *(Sourcebooooks, 2017). She lives in Jerusalem with her husband and children.*

All images used by permission from the artist

Sami Lalu
Jahola

I LEARNED OF Lalu's work from other Qaraqosh refugees in Amman, Jordan, who told me that hidden in their neighborhood lived one of their city's best-known painters. He composed the devotional works that they had grown up with, including those of the famed monastery of Mar Behnam and Sarah. When ISIS invaded, his children scattered to several countries, and he and his wife fled here.

The first time I saw Lalu, he was walking towards the Total gas station in the Hashem al-Shomali neighborhood where we had fixed an appointment, approaching slowly and deliberately. In his late seventies, with white hair, he was carefully dressed in a black suit despite the blistering heat. He greeted me warmly, and then led me back along the street, through a gate and small garden, up a few stairs, and finally into the tiniest of apartments – sparsely decorated and clearly not his permanent home. His wife, Sabiha, greeted him in their variant of Syriac, the dialect of Aramaic that they spoke together. I noticed a few new paintings on the walls, fresh creations in exile. So it was that I began to visit Sami Lalu, so that he might recount to me his decades as a painter in the Nineveh Plains of Iraq.

"WHO IS THAT WOMAN in the painting?" I asked Lalu. The photograph of the portrait *Bride of Qaraqosh* caught my eye immediately as both painting and historical document. The radiant bride stares serenely ahead, adorned in the complete traditional costume of the village of Qaraqosh: a multicolored headpiece embellished with gold jewelry, a blue jacket, a yellow undergarment called a *shokta,* a yellow and black *habria* scarf worn for festive occasions. For the top layer, the bride wears the intricately detailed *shal,* an outer wraparound fabric embroidered with flowers, families holding hands, birds, and colorful lines. In the Nineveh Plains, every village of Christians possesses its own unique traditional costume, donned particularly by older women on weddings and feast days. The *shal* marked a woman as being from Qaraqosh as clearly as a name tag.

"It's my wife!" Lalu exclaimed, and he held the photograph of the painting up against Sabiha's aging face so that I might recognize her.

"I was skinnier back then," she added, laughing. She told me that it was she who had taken the initiative in their courtship. "I saw him," she said, "and I grabbed him for myself." I had to remind myself that the language she spoke with Lalu as she served us tea was in danger of disappearing. Every now and then, his phone would ring with calls from their children, who had resettled in France and Australia, with one remaining in Iraq, and he would put the phone on speaker so that their voices echoed in the room, both gone and still there.

I had expected to be taken by Lalu's religious paintings, but it was his paintings of daily life that drew me in – uncomfortable reminders that such lives can be forever interrupted. The traditional costume reappears throughout Lalu's work. He showed me the photograph of a painting of the village women of Qaraqosh, wearing their traditional dresses and walking beneath a monumental stone arch, the same yellow scarf wrapped around each of their shoulders. The *shal,* this time unadorned, appears again in a third painting of villagers harvesting wheat. In yet another painting, his daughter poses wearing the traditional Assyrian costume of a different Christian village: a headpiece covered with feathers. It was as though Lalu knew, even before the war, that it would be important to capture the

suchness of his world, costumes and details that would disappear as Christians leave.

LALU TRACES HIS LOVE of *suchness* back to his childhood. Born in 1942 in Qaraqosh, he wanted to be an artist from the time he was a boy. "I loved to draw at home," he told me. "I saw how life was beautiful. Everything that I saw, I wanted to replicate." One of the bishops showed him a book with paintings by Michelangelo, Raphael, and da Vinci.

"Might that be possible for me?" the young Lalu asked. His father was a weaver. Many others were farmers, and the village was known for its wheat and barley. It was hard to imagine becoming an artist.

Yet his family encouraged him, and eventually he traveled to Baghdad, where he enrolled at the Institute of Fine Arts to study painting, sculpture, and ceramics. When he returned to Qaraqosh, he became the village's painter and art teacher: Ustez Sami, or Teacher Sami, as a generation of students would call him.

In many ways, Lalu's task was a practical one. As the largest Christian village in Iraq, Qaraqosh contained seven Catholic churches, many of them dedicated to beloved saints largely unknown outside of the region but venerated by the villagers. These churches needed art. Priests commissioned posters for events and devotional paintings: Lalu's was the simple painting of the saint, of the holy family, of Jesus being baptized, in front of which a prayer might be murmured or a candle lit. Whenever a new bishop or patriarch was installed, Lalu was tasked with composing the official portrait. When he wasn't teaching or composing religious art, he painted the members of his family.

Lalu's most visible works were those displayed at the monastery of Mar Behnam

A photograph of Lalu's painting *Al-Hossat in Qaraqosh*

A photograph of Lalu's sketch of the Last Supper

and Sarah in a village outside Qaraqosh, where Christians, Muslims, and Yazidis traveled from the surrounding areas on pilgrimage. Sarah and Behnam, two fourth-century martyrs, had been converted to Christianity by Saint Mattai (Matthew) after Sarah was healed of her leprosy. Their father, King Sinharib the Assyrian, ordered their deaths on learning that his children had become Christians, but later repented and built the monastery near their tomb. The saints were so beloved in the city of Qaraqosh that many children bore their names; a second church within the city proper was also dedicated to them.

For years, Sami Lalu's brother, Monsignor Francis Jahola, was the priest in charge of the monastery. He had encouraged Lalu since childhood, and now he invited him to add several works to the site. On the outside walls, Lalu worked on two white gypsum reliefs – one of Matthew baptizing Sarah, the other of Behnam astride his horse – based on a more ancient engraving within the compound. Inside the church, he completed a painting of the Last Supper, inspired by Leonardo da Vinci's but

time again to the photographs of these lost paintings. Perhaps it is because, bound up as they are in everyday scenes and daily piety, these paintings are reminiscent of a deeper grief, that loss of what Karl Rahner, a Jesuit theologian, calls the "theology of everyday things." It is not the greater losses, but the seemingly smaller ones that seem to haunt those in exile: the lost blessing over a doorway, the dress no longer worn to a wedding, the candle not lit, the particular cup of coffee gone, the local pilgrimage lost. His photographs show that even the most overwhelming grief is expressed most vividly in the particular.

Today, thousands of the Christians of Qaraqosh have resettled around the world, trying to start over in new lands. Others remain refugees in countries like Jordan, hoping for visas. Thousands have also returned to rebuild their city. The churches of Qaraqosh and its environs, too, are being restored, including the monastery. Yet we cannot escape the fact that Christianity in Iraq is on the verge of disappearing.

The last time I went to visit Lalu, his suitcases were packed, and a few weeks later he and his wife left for Melbourne, Australia, where they finally reunited with three of their children. During his final months in Jordan, Lalu had composed one final work: a large painting of Mar Zeina, another saint beloved in Qaraqosh. During our last meeting, he also showed me this painting in the form of a photograph, but not because it had been destroyed by war. Instead, Lalu had asked someone to carry the painting back to Qaraqosh, with the hope that it might be hung in the church of Mar Zeina near his old home, so that a candle might still be lit in front of it, and he might be remembered. ⟶

adapted to reflect the rural Iraqi context. He lived at the monastery for two years, working on the painting. To paint from life, every day he set a table for Jesus and the disciples, placing clay goblets and towels on the olive wood, setting out flatbread baked by the monastery kitchen, filling in the background with walls of Iraqi stone.

"I spent two years working on it," he told me. "Now it's gone."

So, too, is his painting of the baptism of Jesus, as well as the icon-like painting of Mary and child that once hung in a church in Mosul. Yet I have been drawn back time and

Poetry and Prophecy, Dust and Ashes

A review of The Hebrew Bible: A Translation with Commentary, *by Robert Alter*

PHIL CHRISTMAN

Marc Chagall, *Adam and Eve,* detail

IN THE EARLY 1990S, W. W. Norton, that indefatigable supplier of textbooks, invited the literary scholar Robert Alter to assemble a critical edition of Genesis. Alter countered that he'd have to do his own translation, the existing ones being inadequate. Norton agreed. But, Alter tells us in his new treatise *The Art of Bible Translation,* "I had not gotten halfway through the first chapter of Genesis before I discovered that there were all sorts of things going on in the Hebrew, many having to do with its literary shaping, that had not been discussed in the conventional commentaries and that I wanted to take up." The scholar-turned-translator thus found himself launched

on a third parallel career, as commentator. Alter's *Genesis* appeared in 1997 to rapturous reviews, followed by *The David Story* (both Samuels and a smattering of Kings) a few years later, then the Pentateuch a few years after that. Those of us who came to love Alter soon found ourselves in a position akin to that of Robert Caro's or George R. R. Martin's fans. Would he keep going? What if he lost interest, perhaps taking up a less exacting hobby upon his retirement? What if – morbid thought – he died? But twenty-three years after *Genesis,* Alter has completed his work: a finished Hebrew Bible, three volumes lovingly footnoted; an altogether worthier object of contemplation than some

Phil Christman teaches first-year writing at the University of Michigan and is the editor of the Michigan Review of Prisoner Creative Writing. *His work has appeared in* The Christian Century, Paste, Books & Culture, *the* Hedgehog Review, *and other publications. His book* Midwest Futures *(Belt Publishing, 2020) is forthcoming.*

Image from WikiArt (public domain)

fantasy series, or Lyndon Johnson. And I, who am but dust and ashes, review it.

From his earliest writings on the Bible, Alter has warred against what he calls "the heresy of explanation": the tendency among most modern English Bible translators to turn the original text's weirder idioms into their own English-language explanatory glosses. In his introduction to the three volumes, he lists some examples: translations that describe Onan's "offspring" where the text gives us the cruder, but simultaneously far more suggestive, "seed"; avoiding the text's repetition of the metaphorical "hands" (into his hand, in his hand, by his hand, my hand against him) even when this avoidance destroys a careful network of verbal echoes that carry through several chapters; breaking up a large series of actions soldered together into a single sentence by *and* constructions (she did this and that and that and that), or turning several linked simple sentences into compound-complex sentences, and thus slowing a patch of narrative meant to read as a series of quick, decisive actions.

He complains forcefully about this kind of thing in *The Art of Bible Translation,* and sets out a convincing brief guide to some of the Bible's distinct stylistic devices – the semantic parallelism seen throughout the Psalms, in which the first line sets out an idea and the second elaborates or retraces it; the constant use of punning and wordplay, some of it untranslatable; the kind of repetition in which tiny variations or omissions often speak volumes; a preference for concrete language. His translation, however, makes the strongest argument of all. After you've read Alter, the NRSV or the NIV read like the work of a subcommittee of deans. At the same time, he isn't simply literal, in the manner of Everett Fox, whose jerky, jittery rendering of the Pentateuch makes me feel as though I'm reading Talking Heads lyrics. He makes the text sound strange, but still recognizably English. (A brief example, from Isaiah 1:11: "I am sated with the burnt offerings of rams and the suet of fatted beasts." As you read you really feel all those *t*s in your teeth.) In his judiciously-applied literalism and sensitivity to English idiom, he makes possible an encounter with the text that other contemporary translators don't seem to trust readers with.

I don't see myself rereading any other version of the Pentateuch but Alter's in the near future, and any version of the Song of Solomon that avoids the KJV's unfortunate rendering of verse 5:4 ("my bowels were moved for him") is an improvement. At the same time, Alter doesn't fully overshadow the best of his early-modern rivals, Tyndale, Coverdale, and the translators of the KJV. Isaiah 60 is a major literary test for any English Bible translator. In

After you've read Alter, the NRSV or the NIV read like the work of a subcommittee of deans.

his *History of English Prose Rhythm*, George Saintsbury wrote that the KJV's rendering of this passage was "one of the highest points of English prose," and you are probably already murmuring its first verse to yourself: "Arise, shine, for thy light has come, and the glory of the Lord is risen upon thee." (The assonance alone overwhelms – *arise/shine/thy/light* and *is/risen* and *glory/thee*.) Here is what Alter does with it: "Rise, O shine, for your light has come, and the glory of the LORD has dawned over you." I don't know how he could have done better, in modern English; but with the older rendering in your head, you can't help feeling that he's flinched.

THEN AGAIN, when it comes to the Bible, we all flinch. No other book makes me so know my own readerly laziness. I always set out with good intentions, planning to read every verse slowly, sifting every genealogy for hidden theological claims, limning every ritual instruction and temple spec with the empathy of a fieldworker and the ingenuity of an allegorist. I always get through Genesis just fine. At least, that's been true since I read Alter's version back in college – one of a handful of experiences that delivered me from the kind of scared, pious Bible reading that assumes the text is like a lease agreement, too important to be enjoyed. Genesis, in its careful organization, its deft portraiture, its mysteries and silences, most of all its beautifully strange, believably nuanced ending – Joseph, through months of indecision, revealing himself to his brothers via a tortuous and self-torturing process that allows him just enough revenge (can you imagine poor Benjamin, seeing that cup in his bag?) to be believable – is among the loveliest objects in the literary canon. (I want to say that this is self-evidently true, *apart from* religion, *apart from* our assumptions about the truthfulness of the text's worldview, but of course aesthetics and ethics and politics are siblings, like Jabal the herder and Jubal the musician and Tubal-cain the metalworker. They form civilization with continuous reference to each other. And so the aesthetic through which I form a judgment on its loveliness is descended, willy-nilly, from this book.)

My attention will go no further. It turns and rebukes me, like Balaam's ass.

And I always appreciate the weirdness of early Exodus, but then you hit the back half of the book, where God spends several chapters telling Moses *exactly* how to build a temple, and then Moses (or his secretary or, fine, be that way, "the redactor") spends several chapters telling us that that's exactly how he did it, quoting the earlier passages verbatim, page after page, like Kathy Acker in a particularly sadistic mood, and . . . here, reader, my attention will go no further. It turns and rebukes me, like Balaam's ass. Someday, I keep telling myself, I'll find the proper angle of view to see it whole. My patience with the text will attest to God's with me.

Still, these are strange and alien volumes, and by this point the Bible's body count and terrifying strictness have begun to make the alienation more than simply aesthetic. You start to wrestle with a special version of the same problem that worries every theist: if God is all good and merciful, and intends, finally, only restoration and wholeness, then why . . . all this? Why not skip to the good part? You can ask that question about all human history, and about the millennia of death and extinction that preceded human existence, and also about whatever future is left to life. The books themselves provoke such questioning – "Will you really wipe out the innocent with the guilty?" – even as they forbid it – "Who is this who darkens counsel?"

Those doubts only increase with the violence of Joshua, hero to gun-toting colonialists in modern America and modern Israel alike, and Judges, a book that ends in horrifying violence against an unnamed woman. As Israel begins nation-building in earnest ("Give us a king!"), the prophets register their anger at injustice, but they are at least equally insistent about ritual observation and location, a subject about which readers who aren't practicing Jews don't even have the option of having an opinion.

At worst, the picture that emerges for a modern reader is of a God more concerned with setting up elaborate rules than with the Dignity of All People and Concern for Individual Human Lives that thumbnail sketches of Western history often credit these texts with inventing. If God actually isn't like this, then why does God start out by seeming like this? And why inspire a book so easy to misuse? No one has answered this question satisfactorily. No one can. But no one can answer these questions satisfactorily when we pose them about human history, either. The nihilist fails worst of all, since, having explained the slowness and ineffectiveness of the good by refusing to acknowledge its existence, he thus shuts his eyes to more than half of human life.

T IS DEPRESSING, after so many years, to be asking the Bible the same questions I started asking it at eight years old. They are naive ones, but I come by them honestly, having been raised to believe that the Bible could have no mistakes. This hermeneutic could not survive a confrontation with the text's own complexities, its self-contradictions and frank insufficiency as a rulebook for every question. The Bible has a proof text against eating owls, none against molesting children. It tells us that every person shall answer for their own acts, and that their children will pay for the parents' sins. It posits universal brotherhood, then tells Israel to kill all the Amorites. Et cetera. Any village atheist can fill in further blanks. To some extent, the contradiction seems patterned, intentional, as though God liked to make rules in order to break them. Some texts insult eunuchs, others exalt them. Some texts seem to promote a hatred of

everything that isn't Israel, but the whole book of Ruth exists to insert alien blood into David's line. Genesis often seems to justify a world structurally and symbolically situated upon sexual dimorphism, but it also casually lets slip that the first woman came from a man's interior. (In a pinch, a boy can have a womb, and a woman can drive a tent peg through a skull.) Primogeniture is mandated (Deuteronomy 21:17) and yet constantly reversed – Cain is the firstborn, but his worship-offering has something wrong with it. Firstborn sons go on to suffer many comic indignities in the Bible, as befits the national canon of a second-rate military power, soon conquered and colonized. The normal channels for securing and assigning power keep getting dammed up. I wish that God hadn't told the Israelites to put other nations to the ban, but I appreciate that he orders Gideon to stack the deck against himself, again and again, winnowing from an army that already excluded newlywed men (per Deuteronomy) also those who simply didn't feel like fighting (!). Biblical military power, in this story particularly, can seem a thing constituted by its own absence.

The Bible gives us micro-portraits that freeze the heart with recognition.

Biblical inerrancy is a modern doctrine, and these kinds of reactions, too, invite the accusation that I am judging an ancient text by standards not native to it. Indeed, I am. This is a necessary step in a process called "reading." My disgust and confusion are forms of information; they measure my distance from the text's world. A reading that entered fully into the text's thought-world, that required no haggling or silent dissent on the way, would be a useless exercise – you could bring nothing back from it; it would dissolve like a dream. Nor are such objections simply modern. Alter's notes detail many instances in which medieval and early-modern textual critics tried to smooth away the violence and contradictions of the text.

You can make some sense of these things by reading more widely in the literature of the ancient world. It is bad that David butchers so many people, but he is harder to dislike when you've just reread one of Achilles' many "how-dare-you-steal-my-sex-slave-when-I-kidnapped-her-fair-and-square" tantrums. The epics of Gilgamesh or the Atrahasis move us with their portrayal of the inevitability of death, and their proto-Biblical use of repetition (the worm dangling from dead Enkidu's corpse), and the surviving scraps of Canaanite epic poetry fascinate us with their very different treatments of motifs that appear later in the Bible (El's chariot). We certainly appreciate the intermittent concern for widows and orphans that various of these deities express. But the Bible brings a degree of attention to human interiority, and to the feelings of ordinary people, that distinguishes it from every surviving text of comparable antiquity. (The Greek playwrights are its closest rivals.) It has *people* in it. The Bible gives us micro-portraits that freeze the heart with recognition.

I love, for example, the passive-aggressive competition between Leah and Rachel for Jacob's attention, which reaches its height in Genesis 30:14–21. Rachel essentially sells her husband to her sister, for the night, for some mandrakes. Leah, the second-choice bride, finds Jacob as he's on his way home from the fields in the evening, brusquely informs him that she has purchased his services, conceives a baby, and names him Zebulun, remarking,

"God has granted me a goodly gift. This time my husband will exalt me, for I have borne him six sons." In the notes, Alter points out the relevant puns and sound-plays between "Zebulun," "zebed" (gift), and "zabal" (exalt), then glosses the moment thus:

> Having born Jacob half a dozen sons, half of the sanctified tribal grouping of twelve, Leah indulges one last time in the poignant illusion that her husband will now love her.

No other ancient texts give me the tragic and the comic thus blended, in prose that we can only call "realistic."

THIS TERM RAISES the question of genre. The Bible is a library, encompassing epic and saga, poetry and prophecy, but it is also a history. By this I don't mean that every text is literally true – the creation accounts don't even seem intended to be read this way – but that we are meant to think of these stories as accounts of actual people and places, with a smattering of universal history and conjecture to set the stories against a wider background. I was shocked, as a youngster, to realize how profoundly the Bible fails the promises that inerrancy makes for it, but I have been equally shocked, as an adult, to learn how often it frustrates the efforts of biblical minimalists to reduce it to an after-the-fact fantasy composed in exile. Books like James Hoffmeier's *Israel in Egypt* and *Ancient Israel in Sinai* assemble an impressive panoply of evidence that these books, however late they were edited into their current form, contain texts that go pretty far back into history, and engage with material realities (cities, practices) no post-exilic poet could have remembered.

What we are left with, then, is an engagingly, frustratingly, horrifyingly human

Marc Chagall, *Adam and Eve,* oil on canvas, 1912

book, full of misery and violence, of ethnic chauvinism and misogyny, of idealism and generosity and forgiveness and humaneness, of, most of all, genealogies and blueprints. (Make the crossbar of acacia wood! No, dangit, I said *acacia* wood!) It contains much history – biased history, but those terms will always be synonyms, despite the Enlightenment's long imposition of *its* biases. And it contains legends, some of them certainly adapted from the cultures it rejects (see Job, for example). And running through it all, a character too weird to be represented by the text, except from the back, who wrestles us, taunts us, makes us, kills us, and invites us, who are but dust and ashes, to respond. ➔

Editors' Picks

Everything Inside
Edwidge Danticat
(Knopf)

Both Haiti and the Haitian American immigrant experience loom large over these eight short stories by Edwidge Danticat, an acclaimed novelist and *Plough* contributor. This specificity only helps to better sound some universally human chords.

Danticat mines the perils of privilege and charity for riches, as well as our unconscious biases. Which doctor, for example, will prove to be the quack? Infidelity is also a recurring theme – a reality of families torn by the tides of emigration and return.

In "Sunrise, Sunset," a daughter's post-partum depression meets a mother's Alzheimer's in a heartbreaking family crisis that calls forth a deeper love in both.

But most memorable has got to be the final story, "Without Inspection," in which an undocumented construction worker sees his life flash before his eyes in the six and a half seconds it takes to fall five hundred feet (an improbable nine pages, with an even more improbable landing). His employer and the coroner will never know his true name or nationality, but "there are loves that outlive lovers."

Then They Came for Me
Matthew D. Hockenos
(Basic Books)

Martin Niemöller will always be remembered for his much-quoted confession: "First they came for the Communists, and I did not speak out. . . . Then they came for me

and there was no one left to speak for me." This, however, is not the full story. In this biography, Hockenos shows a deeply conflicted Christian leader who initially espoused anti-Semitism and welcomed the rise of the Nazi party as a chance for Christian renewal. It was only after he voted for the Nazis in 1933 that Niemöller gradually recognized his folly and shed his nationalistic sympathies, eventually emerging an outspoken protester of the regime. He was arrested in 1937 and sent to concentration camp.

After the war, Niemöller sought to make amends by devoting the rest of his life to fighting anti-Semitism, nuclear weapons, war, and imperialism. For all Niemöller's flaws, his is ultimately a story of deep repentance and atonement, one that gives hope that anyone can truly change.

A Door in the Earth
Amy Waldman
(Little, Brown)

Rooted in her experiences in Afghanistan as a reporter for the *New York Times,* Amy Waldman has created an engaging novel that vividly describes life in a village in Afghanistan. More importantly, it probes the harm done by Western paternalism and shows how even the most well-meaning intervention can be destructive.

Idealistic and eager to help, Parveen, a young Afghan American anthropology student, travels to a village in the land of her birth. She has been captivated by a book that details the tragedy of women who die in childbirth with little or no medical attention. The author of this book has dedicated himself to building clinics and saving women across Afghanistan. However, the reality Parveen encounters differs widely from the book, which now seems filled with fabrications.

Parveen begins to realize that often outsiders' wish to help is tainted by other desires. "The village was a backdrop against which Americans played out their fantasies of benevolence or self-transformation or, more recently, control." Parveen recognizes this in herself too: she dreams of bringing a young bride with a gift for poetry to the attention of the world – and seeing her own name in print alongside.

Yet Waldman's book raises important questions: If Western intervention can be so harmful, is non-intervention better? How is that different from simply not caring? What actions should we take upon learning of the suffering of others around the globe? *A Door in the Earth* offers no tidy answers, but it does counsel humility. As Parveen discovers, often we can do little – and even when we try to help, we may be the ones who are most changed.

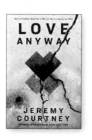

Love Anyway
Jeremy Courtney
(Zondervan)

Jeremy Courtney offers a real-life rejoinder to Waldman's critique – or is it a confirmation? Newlywed Baptists, he and Jessica left Texas shortly after 9/11 to help fight the War on Terror by converting Muslims to Christianity. It wasn't long before these modern crusaders were brought to their knees by their own hubris – and a timely copy of Tolstoy's *The Kingdom of God Is within You*.

Now eager to take Jesus' command to "love your enemies" at face value, the Courtneys asked: What if instead of "preemptive strikes" we offer "preemptive love"? They

found their calling connecting Iraqi children with lifesaving heart surgery, particularly in Fallujah, where environmental toxins left by a US offensive had resulted in a surge of birth defects. Then, in 2014, ISIS arrived, and the Preemptive Love team pivoted to serving the immediate needs of refugees, and then of residents in areas liberated from ISIS control.

Throughout the book, Courtney seems fated to hit all the pitfalls awaiting American do-gooders abroad. Repeatedly the humblebrag is cut short by another face plant. The first night of their aid mission to liberated Fallujah, for example, the Preemptive Love convoy gets stuck to the axles in a sandstorm and is overrun by fleeing ISIS troops, while others on the team suffer an errant American airstrike. Later, they enter Mosul only to be met by tragedy: snipers open fire on those coming to receive their aid, killing a little girl.

Alongside these defeats are moments of moral triumph, as when Courtney's Muslim colleague Sadiq recognizes a shackled detainee as the man responsible for the beheading of Sadiq's best friend. Everyone expects revenge; instead Sadiq offers the man bottled water.

Eventually, though, the horrors of the warzone leave Courtney traumatized. His relationship with his closest coworker breaks down, and so, seemingly, does his faith. Jessica takes the lead in Preemptive Love's next phase, helping Mosul residents rebuild homes and businesses while he minds the kids. The book leaves them there, and leaves the reader asking hard questions about what radical Christianity should look like. Few will match the Courtneys' courage in taking Jesus at his word, even when this meant breaking with Christians back home. Yet how much more could be accomplished, and pain avoided, if they had a committed church community behind them to offer guidance, support, and discernment? ⤞

The Editors

VALOR

A Letter to My Irish Father

MICHAEL BRENDAN DOUGHERTY

L AST YEAR, there was another wedding invitation in my life. This one from Darragh, the cousin I never thought I'd know. As a child he had been a name, but now that you and I are repairing the breach, he is a friend, sometimes a confidant, and a man who will place bets for me. The ones that are not yet legal in America, only in Ireland. He and his household have done well in life, and out of that sense of abundance, he had my whole household come to share in "the big do."

At that wedding, you and I were sharing black beers in the very hotel from which the British shot out the rebels in St. Stephen's Green. My child, your granddaughter, was playing upstairs, perhaps in a room that was used by khaki soldiers as one of the poshest

Faced with a child, you do the things you never thought you would do.

sniper's nests in the history of the empire. A testament that the Irish can accept whatever others dish out. Darragh's wife, I came to learn, was in the touring company for Riverdance. And so we also had testament that night that even Ireland's kitsch can be remade as joy.

And that night you told me your side of one of our stories. You told me about the time you had saved and saved for the plane ticket, only for my mother to disallow you from seeing me after you landed in Newark. She was too upset, she said. And I would be too upset. You went home, having seen your son only for a few minutes.

You told me how, in the following years, your frustration at being unable to see me overcame you. So you researched the times of my recess and lunch at my primary school. And without telling my mother, you flew to America and just presented yourself to me at my school. You made your best friend a coconspirator. He told you he believed you'd both be arrested. You caught so much hell for this from my mother, and from the nuns, and from your own conscience. I had spent years giving you silence, thinking that I was the afterthought in your trip. And here, on this night, I find I was your only thought.

"I felt like a terrorist," you said, recalling it and feeling guilty. The words fell me like a thunderclap. Our estrangement was real, but in that moment, I learned you had made real sacrifices, taken real risks to see me. You would endure any strife it might cause in your house, and any hatred it occasioned in mine. You could barely lift your eyes up to me as you said that now, having a child of my own, I would understand.

I do.

Michael Brendan Dougherty is a senior writer at National Review *and the author of* My Father Left Me Ireland *(Sentinel, 2019), from which this excerpt is taken. He lives with his wife and three children in Mount Kisco, New York.*

Photograph by Robert V. Ruggiero on Unsplash

But I shared with you the other detail of the story, the one that haunted me through all my years of silence. When you had come to the door of my school's cafeteria and my back was to you, that friend of mine said to me, as if it were nothing, "Michael, your dad is here." He had never seen you before. He just looked at you and knew. The simple fact that everyone could see about us – even if, at times, I tried to deny it.

Please, never be ashamed of the things you did to know me and be known by me. No matter how stupid or awful you felt, no matter how strange or upsetting they were to others, even to me. My mother's wish, expressed to you in a letter, was that I should know myself to be Irish. It was an absurd thing to hope for. But maybe a little "terrorism" on your part made it true.

You predicted that my own fatherhood would send me to the roots. Of course it did. Fatherhood makes sense of sacrifice. It is an education that has deepened my ability to be "generous in service, withal joyous." And that is why you and I must, in those small moments we steal now and then in the years we have left, here or in Ireland, make up a little of the time lost between the first time you put the hurl in my hand, and the first time I walked onto a hurling pitch twenty-five years later. My daughter must tramp around in the stony gray soil in Monaghan, where you walked to Mass with your grandparents. She should hear you

argue for Connolly and class war against me, and me argue for Pearse and the nation against you. We can laugh about our common ancestry with the High Kings of Ulster, and all that has gotten us in life. You should bring her a little hurl next time you are here. Get her a Dublin jumper. Better yet, Monaghan. What would your grandfather want for her? "There is only one way to appease a ghost. You must do the thing it asks you" (Patrick Pearse).

You said that our relationship now, as men, is more than you could have rightly hoped. Can't you see that, among all the loves, fears, shames, and uncertainties that belong to us and only us, there is something else that proceeds outward from our relationship? That what we call Ireland is found in the things that pass between us, and reverberate out into the world?

Because, faced with a child, you do the things you never thought you would do. You dare to do what was unthinkable, or even impossible. You become intransigent and indomitable, proud and valiant, yet willing to be the fool, throwing his life away.

I never knew your father. And yet, on the night my daughter was born, I called you with the good news. You may still feel like you have no right to me. And that through your absence in my boyhood, you have forfeited any claim upon your granddaughter. I cannot speak to how you feel. But I can tell you that she has a claim on you. ➤

(continued from page 11)

This notion of life, like the idea of human flourishing, is inescapably normative. It characterizes human beings as particular kinds of creatures whose vitality and happiness depend on their lives being oriented toward certain ends. Here Ruskin departs little from Thomas Aquinas and the Christian tradition in general.

And here is the main friction between Ruskin and the tradition of radical thought that Karl Marx helped to create, a tradition that, despite a host of qualifications, revisions, and objections, still animates the political left. Having abandoned the Romanticism of his youth, Marx also abandoned the fight for a world where the social order reflected an understanding of what people are and what people are for. Without addressing these questions, the search for meaningful work and economic justice Marx focused on led to a dead end. Alienation – the division of human life from human work and human community – became for Marx a stepping stone toward a communist future of large-scale mechanization and emancipation. But emancipation for what? Although Marx remains necessary for anyone who seeks to reckon with the exercise of economic power under capitalism, his later work suffers from this evacuation of meaning. He casts a social vision based on conflict rather than on wholeness, in every sense of that word.

That is one reason I would join with Eugene McCarraher in the hopes that Ruskin's communism would find traction in our moment, when political possibilities are wider than they have been in several generations. His work suggests ways of thinking about work and property where the highest of all the virtues – love, not violence – is the ethic of our economic lives.

Kyle Williams, Charlottesville, Virginia

River Runners

On Christian Woodard's "Who Owns a River?" Summer 2019: "Who owns a river?" That is a provocative question, but one that gets only an indirect answer in Christian Woodard's poignant river-running piece. John Wesley Powell's 1878 call for a communal approach to watersheds, largely ignored by the government then and now, gets the most sympathetic treatment. Yet, as Garrett Hardin reminds us in his famous 1968 essay "The Tragedy of the Commons," shared resources run the risk of being abused by those tempted to maximize personal gains but externalize their costs. Free-market environmentalists often point to Hardin's work as Exhibit A in their quest to get more of the natural world into systems of privatized ownership that will encourage management efficiency (at least from a human-centered standpoint). "It all turns on accounting," they might say. Wendell Berry, however, argued in his 2012 Jefferson Lecture that "It All Turns on Affection." The question of ownership remains up in the air, but Woodard and friends certainly demonstrated their love for the Green River, and that should count for something.

John Murdock, Queen City, Texas

I lived in Southern Idaho and Utah for twenty-one years and never floated the Green River below Twelve Mile. But I spent so many amazing days fly fishing from the Flaming Gorge tailwaters to Twelve Mile – so rich and beautiful. Thank you for sharing the river with me. I read it like I was there.

Bradford Pugh, Mt. Juliet, Tennessee

(continued from page 104)

sea of surging thought & tinted dreams that is in you, all the sky of love and earth of beauty in you, I know from your letters."

He had been writing under the anglicized version of his name, Charles; she convinced him to write under his baptismal name. Once, he told her that he was considering giving up poetry. She protested: "You discover to me the only poetry that has ever satisfied me since I learned to think twentieth century thoughts." They were married in June 1908.

Sandburg worked for several newspapers, and kept writing poetry. His realistic portrayals of the lives of working people and his use of familiar words brought him a devoted audience. "Poetry is a pack-sack of invisible keepsakes," he wrote in 1923. "Poetry is a sky dark with a wild-duck migration. Poetry is the opening and closing of a door, leaving those who look through to guess about what is seen during a moment."

The couple and their growing family – they would eventually have three daughters – moved to Chicago, where Sandburg worked as a reporter for the *Chicago Daily News*. His reporting of the Chicago race riots of 1919 garnered him nationwide appreciation.

The 1920s brought more books of poetry, children's stories, and a two-volume biography of Abraham Lincoln. Sandburg had known Civil War veterans who remembered the president, and had met people who'd been at the fifth Lincoln–Douglas debate, held at his college. "Sprinkled through the speeches of Lincoln," Sandburg wrote, "were stubby, homely words that reached out and made plain, quiet people

> ## "There is a great difference between Christianity and churchianity."
> ### Carl Sandburg

feel that perhaps behind them was a heart that could understand them." The description could have been of Sandburg himself.

On his lecture tours, he would sing American folk songs he'd gathered in his travels, accompanying himself on the guitar. Lloyd Lewis, a newspaper colleague, wrote that when Sandburg sang, "you see farmhands wailing their lonely ballads, hillbillies lamenting over drowned girls, levee hands in the throes of the blues, cowboys singing down their herds, barroom loafers howling for sweeter women, Irish section hands wanting to go home. . . . The characters are real as life, only more lyric than life ever quite gets to be."

Throughout the next decades, he kept writing, kept speaking, responding to each national moment as the troubadour and advocate of the American people. During World War II, he worked on foreign broadcasts for the Office of War Information. The next decades found him in Moscow as a cultural envoy for the State Department; in Washington, DC, meeting with John F. Kennedy in the White House; and participating in the civil rights movement.

He died on July 22, 1967, at his home in Flat Rock, North Carolina. He once observed: "I'll probably die propped up in bed trying to write a poem about America." That was more or less correct.

"Carl Sandburg was more than the voice of America," said President Lyndon B. Johnson, on hearing of his death. "He was America." ⤳

See the visual interpretation of Sandburg's poem "Buffalo Dusk" by Julian Peters on page 62.

Carl Sandburg

JASON LANDSEL

"TRYING TO WRITE briefly about Carl Sandburg is like trying to picture the Grand Canyon in one black-and-white snapshot," wrote his friend and biographer Harry Golden. Here's one such snapshot.

Sandburg was a journalist, poet, folk musician, and fierce advocate for the working class. He published more than forty books and was awarded three Pulitzer prizes and the Presidential Medal of Freedom.

The son of Swedish immigrants, he was born in Galesburg, Illinois, in 1878. He quit school after eighth grade to help support the family, taking work where he could find it: delivering milk, laying bricks.

The bug for travel caught him early. At nineteen, Sandburg hopped a freight train headed west, living as a hobo. After nearly half a year of this vagabond life, he enlisted, serving eight months in Puerto Rico during the Spanish-American War. At the armistice, he returned to Galesburg, enrolling in the local college, where he began, seriously, to write. A professor published Sandburg's first book of poetry, on his own printing press.

He left college without a degree. "I'm an idealist," he wrote. "I don't know where I'm going, but I'm on my way." Once again, he took to the road, selling stereoscopic pictures and giving paid lectures.

Sandburg distrusted organized religion. "There is a great difference between Christianity and churchianity," he wrote. "You can follow Christ without playing tag with the coattails of an ordained preacher." He wrote a poem excoriating the popular evangelist Billy Sunday, who is said to have shot back: "He sounds to me like a Red."

His writing, though, betrays a wrestling with the God who made him, and made America too. "Lay me on an anvil, O God," he wrote in one poem. "Beat me and hammer me into a crowbar. / Let me pry loose old walls. Let me lift and loosen old foundations."

In 1907, Sandburg got a job with the Wisconsin Social Democratic Party, advocating for government reform, the prohibition of child labor and the protection of women in the workplace, a graduated income tax, free medical care for the unemployed, city ownership of utilities, and better working conditions for all.

The evening of his first day of work, December 29, a woman called Lilian Steichen, a dedicated party member and translator of socialist pamphlets, stopped by headquarters to say goodbye to friends on her way back to her teaching job after Christmas. They talked, he saw her to the door, he got her address. In response to his first letter, she wrote:

Do tell me how you contrive to be a moral philosopher and a political agitator at one and the same time – and especially how you contrive to write such poet's English one minute and the plain vernacular the next. The combination is baffling.

Over the next months, they wrote constantly. "The soul of you," Carl wrote to her, "all that

(Continued on preceding page)

Jason Landsel is the artist for Plough's *"Forerunners" series, including the painting opposite.*

Artwork by Jason Landsel